CALIFORNIA *fashion*

# CALIFORNIA *fashion*

## FROM THE OLD WEST TO NEW HOLLYWOOD

### BY MARIAN HALL, WITH MARJORIE CARNE
### AND SYLVIA SHEPPARD

HARRY N. ABRAMS, INC., PUBLISHERS

The authors of this book have been active in the
California fashion industry since the 1940s.
Their common denominator is the Los Angeles Fashion Group International,
as well as being dear friends of
Lynn Norby Johnson,
who was the West Coast editor of HARPER'S BAZAAR from 1951–1988.
Her innate fashion sense and leadership inspired us all,
and it is to her memory that this book is dedicated.

# CONTENTS

1

INTRODUCTION – CALIFORNIA,
*here we come*

An Everyday Crowd on the Beach, Venice, California

A Pepper Driveway in Beautiful California

FOR DECADES CALIFORNIA has been the most important fashion influence of the twentieth century. How odd that almost no one admitted it—certainly not the French, certainly not New York's Seventh Avenue. But the fact remains that more people *dress* in *styles rooted* in CALIFORNIA than styles born almost anywhere else.

Fashion was a passion common to wealthy women in the United States in the early years of the twentieth century. However, they ordered their *haute couture*—made-to-order—gowns from Paris; if time were of the essence, New York's high fashion designers would do, but nowhere else in the United States could the society set shop with confidence.

Paris designers decided *la mode*, and fashion trends started with the rich and trickled

*Opposite:* THESE FIVE BEAUTIES EXPLORED southern California wearing men's hiking boots and cotton shirts accessorized with ties at the neck—this was California casual taken to new extremes. The weather demanded it and so did the sport.

down to the lower classes. Determined to give their customers high fashion at low prices, budget-minded New York manufacturers adapted the trends to clothing that could be sold to the masses.

Meanwhile, the same rich women who were wearing their expensive and highly structured styles from Paris were the very ones who could afford to board the Southern Pacific train bound for the West Coast, where their husbands forked over the few bucks it took to buy land in this refreshing territory with its lush foliage, dramatic mountains, arid deserts, vast beaches, and endless summer. *Southern Pacific lured passengers to California with* SUNSET, *a promotional magazine that advertised free land with a subscription.* Once the tourists were hooked, an automobile was a necessity to enjoy all that southern California had to offer. And with that car came long drives, picnics, hikes, trips to the beach, and the need for casual, comfortable, lightweight clothing—California clothes.

THE AUTOMOBILE QUICKLY became a fixture of California culture, as seen at the beach club at Will Rogers Beach, Santa Monica, 1930.

*Opposite:* SUNSET PACIFIC RAILROAD promoted California with *Sunset* magazine, first published in 1898 to lure passengers and settlers to California. The railroad owned excess land, and in 1910 it promised to give away land (most of it inaccessible at the time) with a subscription to the magazine. Better lots were sold for $19.60, located in what is now the Beverly Glen area of affluent Bel Air.

THE MARCH

# Sunset

THE MAGAZINE of the PACIFIC
AND OF ALL THE FAR WEST

FIFTEEN
CENTS

...EAKING FLYING MACHINE RECORDS
THE INTERNATIONAL AVIATION MEET AT LOS ANGELES

WHEN VENICE BEACH opened in 1905, it was billed as *the* resort town west of the Rockies. Abbot Kinney won the Venice swampland in a coin toss and decided to develop a tourist destination—a "cultural center" that re-created Venice, Italy, complete with canals. He even imported gondolas and real gondoliers, but there the similarity ended. Venice Beach had a midway with circus acts, a Whirling Dervish, a crocodile and alligator farm, a pier with carnival attractions including a roller coaster and bamboo slide, the Pacific Ballroom, an aquarium, a hotel with a rooftop orchestra, and a saltwater plunge.

*Opposite:* By the late '20s Santa Monica, with its wide, beautiful, sandy beach, was dubbed the "Gold Coast." Many movie stars built homes here. Pictured at Constance Talmadge's beach house are Constance, sister Norma Talmadge, Gilbert Roland (Norma's leading man in her first United Artists picture, *New York Nights*), and Constance's husband, Townsend Netcher.

The beach club, Santa Monica Beach.

When Coco Chanel put the word out that *tans were* HOT, *thin was* IN, *and it was* COOL *to look* RELAXED, the contingent of rich women who spent summers in California knew how to achieve what the renowned fashion queen was talking about. At the same time, Fred Cole, heir apparent to a West Coast knitting mill, introduced fashion swimwear—bare legs, shaping for breasts, and dramatically dipping backs. He called them "glamour suits." By 1932 news coverage of the summer Olympics in Los Angeles spread the word that swimsuits were daring in Hollywood.

Hollywood's fan-magazine machine helped to send the message that California had a new way of dressing. Sure there was glamour, the kind movie stars represented. But more important was *casual wear, the kind of clothes* that made for EASY LIVING AND FUN, worn by everyone—including movie stars. Active sportswear—tennis dresses and golf clothes—found their way into magazines. International swimsuit trends developed as actresses played at the beach in the newest looks and movie-magazine photographers snapped their images. Photographers also took pictures of celebrities dressed in hiking gear as they trekked through local mountains. Fashion history was in the making.

Women's high fashion in the 1930s consisted of dresses with big shoulder pads—as worn by Joan Crawford and Bette Davis in the movies and created by Gilbert Adrian on his Hollywood drawing board in 1932. The broad-shouldered look caught on and every French and New York runway featured the style. News was spreading to watch California style.

Suddenly California clothing manufacturers realized that what was happening in their own backyard was having an impact nationally and internationally. A select corps of buyers from elite Eastern stores began heading west, scouting new looks in comfort clothes that would impress their wealthy customers.

CHRISTIE BRINKLEY, California girl. "The legs are longer, the eyes clearer, the skin more exuberant. A combination of maximum looks and minimum restraint, that tranquil body and restive psyche—that is the California Girl."—Tim Tyler, *Time* magazine, 1969

Meanwhile, during World War II, working women began wearing the blue denim overalls that Levi Strauss had introduced to Gold Rush California in 1873. While men were fighting in Europe, women took over factory jobs and needed work clothes. Jeans—as they came to be called—were comfortable, and they certainly looked good.

Riding the zeitgeist, manufacturers banded together and started paying to bring large groups of buyers and press to California, hoping for newspaper publicity that would showcase fashion news from the West. A consortium of manufacturers, called California Fashion Creators, wined and dined their influential guests, treating them to all the West had to offer: the beaches, the movies, the gardens, the hills. The plan was to merge fashion and a way of life, to show why the California look was what the rest of the world silently craved. The technique worked: America began paying attention. California was about fashion on the streets, CLOTHES THAT SUITED A *lifestyle*, although no journalist had yet used that word. For the first time in history, fashion was not about what rich people wore, not about what designers were pushing, but rather about what real people wanted to wear for real life. If trends had always trickled down, they were suddenly trickling up . . . from the streets of California.

All—whether acid-washed, bleached, preshrunk, stone-washed, deconstructed, patchworked, decorated, studded, jeweled, feathered, ribboned, painted, ripped, body-hugging, monster-sized, capri-cut, cargoed, bellbottom, carpenter-looped, boot cut, hip-hugging, or cropped—stem from the original jeans that Strauss brought to the gold country. All—whether acid-washed, bleached, preshrunk, stone-washed, deconstructed, patchworked, decorated, studded, jeweled, feathered, ribboned, painted, ripped, body-hugging, monster-sized, capri-cut, cargoed, bellbottom, carpenter-looped, boot cut, hip-hugging, or cropped—stem from the original jeans that Strauss brought to the gold country.

2

*there's gold in those*

BLUE denims

TODAY, THE LEVI 501® jeans and jackets have been elevated to a new status of vintage collectibles. Connoisseur Zip Stevenson of "Denim Doctors," who buy, sell, and repair vintage jeans, points out the criteria for collectible jeans—the true indigo color and how it has mellowed, the character, and the degree to which it shows wear, i.e., the horizontal creases known as "whiskers" on the leg of the pant or the sleeve of a jacket.

*Above:* Levi Strauss 501® jeans will continue to be in the vernacular of the twenty-first century. Levi® jeans have gone from gold-bearing mine to firm, to ranch, and to status-ranking fashion with international appeal. From miners to presidents, the blue denim Levi's® have traveled a long road to become the most copied and coveted kind of covering. Photo by Fergus Greer

WHEN DESIGNER Bill Blass wrote in *The New Yorker* about "American Gals," the long-reigning king of old-guard East Coast chic acknowledged that "Nothing any fashion designer has ever done has come close to having the influence of blue jeans. THAT LEVI STRAUSS INVENTION— ONE OF THE sexiest ITEMS A MAN OR A WOMAN CAN WEAR— is the most significant contribution America has made to fashion. And, after all, it's based on the most chic and least contrived American icon—the cowboy."

Levi Strauss didn't have fashion or cowboys on his mind when he constructed the first denim pants back in 1873. Rather, he was after the money that pure function could bring. By the time he came to California in 1853, he was focused on the Gold Rush. But unlike most people around him, he was not there for the gold that was washed from the streams but for the possibility of the golden profits that would come from supplying the miners with dry goods. His future partner Jacob Davis approached him with the idea of making denim pants with rivets in 1872. Those pants turned out to be comfortable and durable for the miners, who spent days hunched over, panning the water for sparkling rocks.

Denim, as the fabric of these destined-

to-be-legendary pants was called, dates back to the sixteenth or seventeenth century. Some claim denim came from the French city of Nimes (*de Nimes*, as the French would say); others say it was first made in Genoa (where the Italians called it "jean" cloth). Originally woven of silk and wool in France, and cotton, linen, and wool in sixteenth-century Italy, by the eighteenth century the all-cotton version of the fabric was firmly established as a staple. It was the most durable cloth in the world—material that "breathed" while still withstanding thousands of washings, and the more it faded, the better it looked. Its qualities were perfect for the needs of Strauss, whose customers would spend most of their days in a natural washing machine.

Adding copper rivets at stress points

became a patented process that Strauss and Davis used to distinguish their wares. (Although the crotch was certainly a stress point for these bent-over miners, the rivet strategically placed there was removed years later, after too many burns were reported by cowboys who squatted around the campfires.)

What people on the streets did in their dungarees has determined the longevity of the pants. Denims have become symbolically linked to lifestyle from their earliest days. And the fact that jeans could become de rigueur for people of all economic levels has made them the world's most worn and most talked-about piece of clothing. First associated with the working classes, jeans have shown up on the lower bodies of upper-echelon folk as well. Nancy and Ronald Reagan were always clad in denim pants when they tended their Western White House ranch near Santa Barbara, Jimmy Carter and Rosalyn wore them on their peanut farms, and the Clintons wore them to school. Brigitte Bardot turned jeans into sex-kitten garb when she curled up at her French home. The jeans that Marilyn Monroe wore in one of her films and then donned for Hollywood shopping trips were auctioned at Christie's and sold to Tommy Hilfiger $42,000.

The *cowboy* put his stamp of approval on LEVI'S ® JEANS while working the cattle ranches of California. The tough blue

JOHN WAYNE AND Gary Cooper were cowboy heroes of the silver screen.

*Opposite:* HOPALONG CASSIDY (William S. Boyd), the real cowboy who did all his own riding and stunts in competition rodeos and Hollywood films.

denim could withstand the constant friction of his leather saddle, while he was surveying the rough-and-tumble landscapes of California's early Mexican-held ranchos. Other cowboys caught on, and the durable trouser showed up on every precursor to the Marlboro Man. As Hollywood began to capture real cowboys on film in the persons of Tom Mix and William S. Hart, the fact that they wore Levi's® jeans created a tradition for latter-day screen dudes such as John Wayne, Gary Cooper, and Randolph Scott. When Will Rogers became the people's choice for president of the United States, it was because they could relate to his denim-clad Everyman persona and his cowboy wit. Singing cowboys such as Gene Autry and Roy Rogers teamed fancy Western shirts with their basic jeans, as did Hopalong Cassidy, the Lone Ranger, and even Howdy Doody. It was only when a man named Nudie Cohn (a non-cowboy from Manhattan who came to Hollywood to put rhinestones and spangles on Western wear and reached royalty stature in the world of cowboy clothes) turned cowboy outfits into dress-up wear that designers around the world were actually inspired to look at denims and other Western fashion in a new light.

It took more than cowboys to attract the world to jeans, however. Hippies had their hand in the movement too. San Francisco's flower children of 1960s Haight-Ashbury

RONALD AND NANCY REAGAN were identified with ranch life at Rancho del Cielo in Santa Inez Valley, which became known as the Western White House, where they entertained friends and dignitaries.

used their jeans as a canvas to make fashion statements as well as political ones. While London was caught up in mods and rockers, New York was still into preppy, and Paris was reeling from the haute-couture success of young designers such as Yves St. Laurent and Courrèges, San Francisco and Los Angeles were dressing for a music revolution and a philosophical revolution that would change the world. Indeed, peace symbols and holes in the knees adorned the same pair of pants, ribbons regaled the seams, and messages like "Make Love, Not War" were embroidered on bottoms. Jeans became the love generation's uniform. The same kids would age to be called Baby Boomers and Yuppies, but even as their music and their politics changed, they would never lose their love for jeans. And before long, the mods and rockers (read the Beatles and the Rolling Stones), Yves St. Laurent, and Brooks Brothers would all be hailing the power of blue denim pants.

The 1997 ad campaign for Levi's® jeans stated, "Ralph wore them"; "Calvin wore them"; "Tommy *wore* them." Designer Geoffrey Beene corrected this, saying, "Ralph stole them, Calvin stole them, and Tommy *stole* them." Almost every designer worth his or her label has adapted Levi's® jeans for their customers— from Tom Ford and his $3,000 Gucci jeans to the unknown designer of Lee jeans on the

El Paso/Mexican border. All—whether acid-washed, bleached, preshrunk, stone-washed, deconstructed, patchworked, decorated, studded, jeweled, feathered, ribboned, painted, ripped, body-hugging, monster-sized, capri-cut, cargoed, bellbottom, carpenter-looped, boot-cut, hip-hugging, or cropped—stem from the original jeans that Strauss brought to the gold country.

During the last three decades of the twentieth century, jeans belonged completely to the people. The Gap—once "merely" a Levi's® jeans store devoted to the generation gap that jeans helped eliminate, at least when it came to clothes—was dressing the world at an affordable price, with Gap jeans in every style and size imaginable. And the streets of big cities were populated with kids who rebelled against such a uniform look, deciding that they should define themselves by the seat of their pants. It sank lower and lower on their hips, the legs got wider, the fit got baggier. Baggies became the look that would close a century, a look from the streets that would defy gravity as well as convention. It would put youth in the driver's seat of fashion, and dare adults to try and understand. These kids would wear the jeans Levi Strauss had created. But they would wear them their way.

Haute-couture designers around the world, such as Gucci (above), have restyled jeans in every shape and color.

35

SWIMSUITS OF THE '60s: Carol Christensen in slit-front suit by Rudi Gernreich, $25;
Ruta Lee in green-check cotton bikini by Rose Marie Reid; Jill St. John in Rose
Marie Reid blue back-button tank suit, $24; Stephanie Powers in Rudi Gernreich
patchwork knit suit with plastic belt, $24; Joan Blackman in Catalina white rib;
Silo in Elisabeth Stewart two-piece cotton print, $20; Barbara Eden in Cole yellow
knit bikini, $16; Julie Payne, in forefront, in Catalina black-dotted bikini, $13.

In Boston, circa 1907, *Australian aquatic champion Annette Kellerman was promptly arrested for showing up on the beach in an "indecent" one-piece knitted bathing suit that covered her from shoulder to ankle but was so tight-fitting it completely revealed her shape. In California the immediate response was for women to appear on the southern* California seashore wearing an abbreviated version of Kellerman's look with shortened legs and a lower neckline—and just dare the cops to complain. But somehow even a briefer version of those black and gray wool-knit swim costumes that had migrated from the East Coast looked very wrong to the dis-criminating sun lovers at Santa Monica Beach. The smelly, wet wool and the warm California sun were a bad combination.

Of course these new, swimmable suits were a vast improvement over the ruffled and layered silk or linen pantaloons of the late 1800s and the flounced sailor dresses of the early 1900s that made their way to the sand. After Kellerman offered up her silhouette

and sought freedom as an active woman, it was a short leap to 1926 when renowned swimmer Gertrude Ederle cut up her one-piece swimsuit into a very freeing bra and shorts ensemble and then swam the English Channel wearing just these bare essentials. Crossing the Channel in just fourteen hours and thirty-one minutes, Ederle became the first woman to accomplish the feat and beat the men's record.

Both Kellerman and Ederle found brief fame in motion pictures because the savvy producers of films knew that swimming was one sure way to justify exposing a woman's body on the big screen without wrangling with censorship issues. Now that Hollywood needed swimsuits, it only took a savvy fashion marketer to fill the need and offer fashionable water wear to the general public. Enter Fred Cole, whose family owned a long-underwear manufacturing company called Westwood Manchester Knitting Mills. When he took over in 1925, his competitors—the highly successful Pacific Knitting Mills in Los Angeles operated by Ed Stewart (who would later change the company's name to Catalina) and Jantzen Knitting Mills in Oregon—had already begun manufacturing swimsuits on their underwear machines, capitalizing on the growing needs of an increasingly active American public. Catalina had emerged in 1916 with a flying fish as its logo on swimwear,

and Jantzen, which had made its first suit in 1913, adopted a little diving girl complete with cap and stockings as its imprimatur. Both were leaders in the small swimwear market—albeit making dull, wool, one-piece suits that did everything to downplay a woman's assets.

Cole, himself a not-too-successful actor, realized that Hollywood wanted colorful swimsuits with sex appeal and, by extension, so did American women. He quickly put his showman talents to work and created the business that would suddenly become California's claim to fame: *the fashion swimsuit.* Thinking of his swimsuits the way other designers thought of evening gowns in the Roaring Twenties, Cole first turned to the influence of California's desert, sea, sky, and flowers, introducing colors such as sand, coral, aqua, blue, rose, yellow, and geranium.

When he ventured to Macy's in New York on a dreary, rainy Christmas Eve in 1925, Cole spread out his colorful, flower-motif suits with their relatively skimpy silhouettes. The buyer registered shock and then

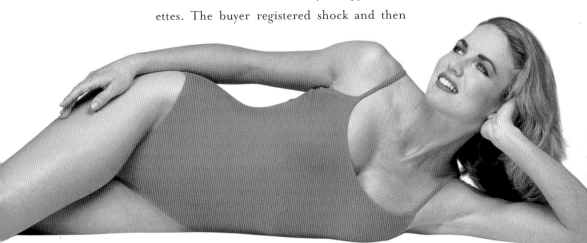

delight. She ordered thousands in the full array of colors. Cole returned with orders in hand, shipped and delivered the suits in January instead of June, creating the "resort season" in department stores (to explain the need to consumers for buying swimsuits in January). Only years later would Cole admit that he was so desperate for money that year that he had shipped the suits early so he could collect his payment quickly.

Because Macy's had responded so well to his fresher, barer looks, Cole scooped the back of his suits as low as decency would allow—then dipped it a bit more. By 1927 he had shortened the legs of the suits to the top of the thigh and plunged the neckline, dubbing them "Hollywood Swimsuits." Following

Macy's lead, swimsuit buyers nationally began to buy Cole's designs. In a few years, rather than waiting for Cole to head east with his newest styles, the store buyers took advantage of the excuse to go west.

As the buyers filtered into southern California looking for stylish swimwear, more local manufacturers realized that Cole was onto something big with his high-fashion swimwear concept. Swimsuit designers at Cole, Catalina, and Mabs of Hollywood played an important role in the growing industry, incorporating technological innovations to improve the suits not just in form but also in function. Soon CALIFORNIA was recognized as the swimwear capital of the world, and the heads of swimsuit companies became the leaders of a burgeoning California fashion empire.

The timing was good. The world was beginning to understand that California—and especially Los Angeles—was unique. The 1932 OLYMPICS pushed southern California into the limelight, as newspapers, magazines, and movie newsreels focused on Los Angeles not just as the site of the Olympics but as a place where the living was easy, the landscape was magical, and the CLOTHES were comfortable, glamorous, and geared to an outdoor life. This was the place of Hollywood and movie stars, money and swimming pools. This was the life everyone

Opposite: THE 1932 WOMEN'S Olympic Swim Team is honored at the Agua Caliente Race Track.

dreamed of attaining. And if buying a California-made swimsuit meant having a piece of the glorious life, so be it.

The increased attention, however, was propelling California into the swimsuit limelight in the first half of the twentieth century. Adventurous minds were constantly creating new looks that took advantage of the sun and sand that defined the state. Cole's designer Margit Fellegi bared the midriff in 1939. But a few years later, Mabs Barnes, who had participated in the '32 Olympics in Los Angeles as a discus thrower, joined forces with her new husband, an underwear salesman, to create Mabs of Hollywood. When they clad actress Joan Blondell in a flesh-colored swimsuit, it became front-page news around the world. But for years, no one out-bared Jo Lathwood, the wiry swimwear designer who would freelance at Catalina during the high design season, only to finance her trips to Europe and the South Pacific where she spent six months of every year. On a trip to France after World War II, she discovered women wearing minuscule swimsuits on the beach. Named after a French atoll in the South Pacific, the FRENCH *bikini* made its debut in a French fashion show at the Molitor pool in 1946. Lathwood designed the first California bikini and what became *the* style of Santa Monica Beach, a few steps from Lathwood's studio.

Lathwood's bravado established California's beaches as the place to showcase bodies. It also helped position California at the forefront of experimental design. The groundwork was laid for other experiments in body baring. It took years for the rest of America to accept the brevity of Lathwood's bikinis, despite the fact that the style would be adopted and adapted by manufacturers throughout the swimwear industry.

The postwar economic boom allowed more Californians to have swimming pools. The swimming pool became the singular icon of success, beauty, and glamour. And if you had a pool, you had pool parties. The California swimsuit industry began creating glamorous bathing suits, with accessories such

as matching skirts to create casual cocktail attire. Rose Marie Reid, one of the legends in the swim apparel business, created the first gold lamé suit for "at-home wear," for California hostesses entertaining guests; she used swimmable velvets and beaded fabrics, fashioning stoles and jackets and shirts that were the makings of a poolside wardrobe. Originally a sponsor of the Miss America Pageant in Atlantic City, in 1951 *Catalina* became the cosponsor of the Miss Universe contest, making the swimsuit competition one of the most important aspects of the event. Catalina tapped the talents of its long-

time designer Mary Ann DeWeese to outfit the beauty contests' participants, sending the designer to personally fit each contestant in a swimsuit. She left Catalina later the same year to establish her own swimsuit company.

Whether it was Esther Williams in the 1940s, Marilyn Monroe and Jayne Mansfield in the 1950s, or Annette Funicello and Sally Field in the 1960s, the big screen turned swimwear into big business. Movie stars taught us that it was okay to go bare, as long as there was water nearby. By the mid-1960s, the bikini had been established as a classic.

In 1952 Rudi Gernreich, a futurist whose designs were often misunderstood,

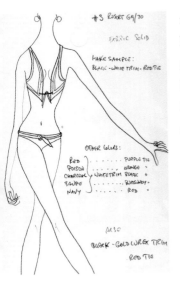

removed all inner construction, engineering his wool knitted maillots for shaping the bust, giving women the freedom to swim without being poked by the metal wires and bones that had supported other "uplift" designs. Always steps ahead of other swimwear designers, Gernreich made a habit of shaping swimsuits that were radically different from other designs; his were classified as swimwear couture, the best and brightest in 1960s California. An artist who was always eager to make a grand sociological statement—and gain notoriety—Gernreich saw the changes of the 1960s and asserted that soon women would be dressing without tops. To prove his point, in 1964 he designed the monokini: a swimsuit with no top. The *topless* bathing suit, as it was called, was composed of knitted boy shorts held up by suspenders.

No swimsuit would garner as many inches of press coverage as Gernreich's topless— more inches, indeed, than the suit itself possessed. The pope banned it. Police arrested the nineteen-year-old who dared to wear it to the beach (and then demanded a male jury). And the incredibly endowed Carol Doda would dance in it at her notorious Condor Club in San Francisco. Although the life of the topless bathing suit was short and very few women ever owned one, its legend has outlived its creator. And the staying power of the thong, another Rudi Gernreich design

from 1974 (too often credited to the beaches of Brazil where it first was photographed in 1975), is reinforced in every new underwear and swimsuit catalogue.

It was decades after Gernreich's topless design had become a classic that another California innovation would make an even bigger impression on the world. A new look in swimwear hit the pages of *Elle* and *Vogue* magazines in 1986, changing the face of swimwear—and street fashion—for years to

GERNREICH'S TOPLESS BATHING SUIT, modeled by Peggy Moffitt.

come. The brainchild of swimwear designer Robin Piccone, the new suits were made of neoprene, a combination of rubber and nylon. Piccone designed an entire collection for a small dive-wear manufacturer in Hermosa Beach called Body Glove. HER ZIP-UP ONE-PIECE SUIT AND DERRIERE-CUPPING STRAIGHT SKIRTS (*designed to wear over the swimsuits*) STARTED A REVOLUTION IN BODY-HUGGING CLOTHES that caught on in the ready-to-wear fashion world. The all-female rock group the Go-Go's wore the neon-colored swim clothes on stage, and before long the swimwear turned up on dance floors all over the country. Soon neoprene was the fashion fabric of the moment, opening the door for lighter-weight spandex-blend clothing. Piccone's designs were considered so revolutionary that her two original neoprene swimsuits and the after-swim skirt are included as part of the collection of the Costume Institute of The Metropolitan Museum of Art in New York. Like Gernreich's designs, Piccone's swimwear mirrored a changing sociological view of women. Hers symbolized the females of the 1980s as strong, athletic individuals who were ready to dress to reflect that image. The major difference between her work and Gernreich's was that the masses started wearing her styles on the beach and off.

When *Baywatch*, a television show filmed on the beaches that stretch from Malibu to

Redondo in southern California, became one of the most watched shows in the world, California's impact on the swimsuit world peaked again. Stylists for the show combed the shops and swimsuit studios of the greater Los Angeles region in search of each week's perfect suits, worn by Pamela Anderson and other perfectly proportioned women and men. Those styles influenced swimwear the world over.

Honolulu, Tahiti, Ft. Lauderdale, Rio de Janeiro, the Côte d'Azur are all beach havens, but none has had the lasting fashion power that the California swimwear empire created and has maintained for the better part of a century.

SPEEDO DEVELOPED FASTSKIN™, a full-body swimsuit combining a new fabrication like the skin of a shark and a revolutionary design, making it scientifically the fastest swimsuit for competitive swimming, modeled by Olympic Gold Medalist Lenny Krayzelburg and Amy Van Dyken.

THE BABES OF TV's *Baywatch*.

BAYWATCH

ESTHER WILLIAMS WEARING a suit by
Mabs of Hollywood, 1942.

SWIMWEAR MANUFACTURING is a very
specialized industry because of technology and short delivery time. A
turning point in the industry came in
1993, with the merger of many brand
and licenses, which are now designed,
produced, and sold under one roof.

THIS BLOUSON SWIMSUIT by Bette
Beck of Elisabeth Stewart
Swimwear won the *Sports
Illustrated* Design Award in 1962.

JO LATHWOOD'S 1940s bikini on
the runway of the California
Designing Women's show in
1976.

Today more than 50 percent of all swimwear is produced in California, including eastern labels such as Polo, Oscar de la Renta, Anne Klein, Nautica, and Liz Claiborne, along with California labels such as Cole, Catalina, and LaBlanca.

A BIKINI FROM the Spring 2002 collection of BCBG Max Azria.

A DENIM BIKINI by OP (Ocean Pacific), 2000.

RUDI GERNREICH'S UNCONSTRUCTED (cut to show the body) maillot in wool jersey in 1952, modeled by his house model Jimmy Mitchell.

ONE OF THE BEST-KNOWN labels in San Francisco was Koret of California, whose designer, Stephanie Koret, launched several fashion firsts such as permanently pleated cotton and Koraset carefree fashions. Koret, with their Napa Valley and Jax Sportswear divisions, was purchased in 1999 by the Kellwood Company. Advertisement, circa 1950.

FROM ITS EARLIEST DAYS, *California* was accustomed to innovation. The pattern that Levi Strauss and the forward-thinking swimsuit designers had set proved that if the state was to be recognized for anything, it would be for being first with a new idea.

In the 1930s and 1940s, New York designers were doggedly reliant on inspiration that came from Europe, out of respect, habit, and practicality. Europe, especially France, had long been the magnet for the best fashion minds, and thus anyone who dared stray from a European trend risked negative reviews from the fashion press. As New York's renowned Claire McCardell admitted about her work in the 1930s and early 1940s, "I did what everybody else did, copied Paris."

Not so in California. What was the point? The European knockoffs that filled the stores were inappropriate for *the West,* where the weather called for lighter fabrications and the LIFESTYLE demanded freedom of movement and a casualness that couldn't be found in the formal, traditional collections. The thirst for relaxed dressing was quenched when Lou Van Roy introduced sportswear separates—clothes more casual than dresses cinched at the waist and zipped or buttoned up the back—in the early 1930s. Working for a company called Lou Kornhandler, Van Roy showed women that a skirt and jacket purchased separately

A PANTSUIT BY LOU VAN ROY, one of the earliest designers of separates.

could be worn together or with other items in the wardrobe; that pants weren't just for men; and neither, for that matter, were vests. She promoted the concept of comfortable clothes and reinforced it when she offered "peon pants," a style of wrapped bottoms that were modeled after styles worn in Mexico by peasants. She interpreted the look in vivid California colors, and a trend was born. Taking pants to another dimension, she created the first casual slacks suit, and then shortened the pants to create culottes and playsuits. Playsuits were originally designed by Marjorie Montgomery—her styles predated the playsuits designed by McCardell, the solitary New Yorker who gained fame with her collections of casual clothes. McCardell was also said to have been the first designer to make clothing in unpredictable materials, such as mattress ticking, a fabric she used for trousers that were modeled on Lauren Bacall in 1943. But it was actually Los Angeles–based playclothes designer Marjorie Montgomery who ventured into mattress ticking and sun-bleached denim fabrications in the mid-1930s.

The outdoor lifestyle in southern California meant women, and especially young women, had trim bodies that needed smaller sizes than the well-padded bodies common in the East. To meet this demand, Peggy Hunt, who had made a name for herself designing lace-detailed cocktail dresses in the Holly-

PEGGY HUNT, "Lady of the Lace," earned that title with her collections of cocktail and evening dresses (and under the Jean Carol label, a moderately priced line). Her illusion necklines seemed more revealing than they were—always ladylike, as is this black lace evening gown worn by model Jimmy Mitchell, who would later become a Rudi Gernreich house model.

# PEGGY HUNT

wood glamour tradition, invented "junior" sizes in 1930. At first designed to fit her daughter Jeannette, the clothes appealed to executives at Bullocks Wilshire—the poshest retailer in town—who asked Hunt to create a collection of day dresses cut to the new, narrower body type: smaller bustline, shorter waist, narrower shoulders. These newly sized clothes went into the "Collegienne" department. Other retailers across the country accepted the concept as a way to dress high-school and college-aged girls who had not yet developed more mature figures. Two years later one of Hunt's employees, Helen Gudgell, opened her own collection: sportswear sized to fit juniors.

By 1945, a year after Los Angeles's Dede Johnson designed the tapered, chopped-length pant that grazed the calf and came to be known as "pedal pushers" (and much later the "capri"), ultra-casual sportswear had taken hold as street fare, not just in the West, but all over the world. Johnson (whose ownership of the pedal-pusher design had been disputed by swimwear designer Mary Anne DeWeese, who also took credit for the popular style) followed up in 1946 with wide, short pants called "clam diggers"; the "cloud stroller," a divided skirt suit to be worn for air travel on the new jets; and trouser skirts, all variations on the skirt that made sense in California.

New York and European manufacturers

sold short "resort" wear collections, a concept necessitated by the winter-escape vacations that wealthy Europeans and East Coasters took, and their designers took long, hard looks at what designers such as Johnson and Van Roy were doing. Californians lived the "resort" life year round—at least from a weather perspective—they reasoned, so the casual, light-weight clothing designed for life there was worth copying. When legs got into the freedom of short pants, whether in Los Angeles or Brooklyn, they never got out.

In the same comfortable vein, as early as 1932, Irene Bury, a housewife who intended to "prove I was capable of making my own living," convinced her husband that there was a call for "lounging" pajamas, comfortable clothes to wear around the house. The idea of clothes that were comfortable—not uptight, like most of the clothes that were coming out of New York—caught on so fast in California that before long Bury was reinterpreting the pajamas in fabrics that could be worn while entertaining or at the beach. Corduroy loungers in combinations of two, three, and four colors were her first offering. Then came a burlap-type fabric she called "Lana-cloth"—a fabric so cheap that it was used for bagging flour; reinterpreted for clothing, this soft cotton was a Depression-era solution to fabric shortages that became a new trend.

By 1940 comfortable clothes were expect-

ADDIE MASTERS EARNED the title of California fashion's "hostess with the mostest" with her glamorous at-home fashions, such as these silk pajamas.

ed from California designers. Agnes Barrett introduced the *"broomstick" skirt,* the tightly pleated, tiered skirt that never showed wrinkles (an idea she had borrowed from the Navajo squaws). Barrett devised a way of wetting the skirt, twisting it to wring the water out of it, and wrapping the twisted bundle around a broomstick to dry, thus creating its name and its multiple pleats. The casual skirt took the worry of wrinkles out of wearing skirts, and the pleating allowed a slim look without sacrificing the length of a stride or the ease of getting in and out of a car.

Although the broomstick skirt had an ethnic look, relaxed and vividly colored, it was not as identifiably early Californian or Latino in its inspiration as the designs of Louella Ballerino. The designer, who had studied the arts and crafts of Hispanic cultures, opened her own company in 1938, selling separates styled of rustic fabrications, some embroidered, some embellished with colorful ribbons, and still others trimmed with little square wood blocks. Her off-the-shoulder blouses worn with ethnic-inspired skirts were a vivid interpretation of the Mexican influence in California. Her work was featured in the pages of *Vogue* and *Harper's Bazaar* alongside the work of Claire McCardell, one of the early indications that California designers were at last gaining national respect for their contributions to American fashion.

A contemporary of Ballerino, Addie Masters recognized that one of the unique aspects of life in California was the ability to entertain outside on the patio. With that thought in mind, in 1940 she took off on Irene Bury's hostess pajama idea and created pants with hems that were three to six yards around. Initially a national success, the pants quickly became an affront to the war effort and had to be limited to nineteen inches around to meet the government restrictions on fabric use. Her trimmer PJs were the first styles that fashion-forward Bullocks Wilshire advertised as "government-controlled" fashions. The public had come to expect comfortable clothes from Masters, and she ventured into daytime dresses that wrapped around the body and tied at the waist, a style she called the "wrap rascals" (later reinterpreted by New Yorker Diane von Furstenberg, first in the 1970s and again in the late 1990s). Masters's original design was as relaxed and as close to sportswear as a dress could get and still be called a dress.

Designers in Los Angeles started rethinking the concept of sportswear with an eye toward expanding the category. In 1945 stylists such as Irene Saltern, a pioneer in the "coordinated sportswear" market, began merchandising her designs, making it easy for the consumer to purchase not just one garment but three or four at the same time, all

designed to work together. To create coordinated sportswear separates, as they are still
called in the retail industry, designers worked
with fabric houses to color-coordinate solids,
prints, and woven patterns from which various skirts, pants, blouses, jackets, and tops
could be styled, then the pieces were mer-
chandised to *mix and match* to create different ensembles that would expand a
woman's wardrobe and flatter different figure
types. This was perhaps *the single most important
innovation in the history of American sportswear.*
When the concept of coordinated sportswear
was introduced to the American woman,
shopping for clothes was never again the same
experience. Pre-coordinated pieces allowed
women to wear clothes comfortably and
remain confident that the pieces worked
together. The plan allowed retailers to
depend on the fact that a customer was going
to easily rationalize spending more money on
the components of an ensemble than she
would on a single dress.

All of these fashion firsts in California
might have gone unnoticed had it not been
for the doors opened by the clever marketers
in Los Angeles's swimwear industry, the manufacturers who saw the financial benefit of
herding the buyers—and the press—out to the
West to see what was happening in the design
rooms. Following their lead, individual
clothing manufacturers banded together to

ANOTHER DIMMITT "FIRST"

PERHAPS THE MOST unusual of the Affiliated Fashionists in her designs for weathering "liquid sunshine" was VIOLA DIMMITT. "Rain, rain, go away" was not in her vocabulary, for her success grew out of her satin-backed rayon raincoats. This satin-back trenchcoat was designed in the early 1940s.

invite buyers to shows of their collections. The first of these groups was the Affiliated Fashionists, eight of the talented women who had been designing in a vacuum, free of the European influence: Agnes Barrett, Louella Ballerino, Peggy Hunt, Marjorie Montgomery, Addie Masters, Irene Bury, Mabs Barnes of swimwear fame, and Viola Dimmitt, a woman who had introduced the concept of a lightweight raincoat that was styled like a coatdress and sold more than 150,000 units. The Fashionists, active as a group from 1926 to 1960, had a common cause: communicate to buyers and the press that the look of California was new and that it suited the changing lifestyle of America and the changing mindset of the American woman. Together they acted as unofficial hostesses who entertained visiting retailers, but more important, they offered combined showings of their collections to make certain that stores all over the country carried California merchandise.

In 1937 a Los Angeles–based magazine and newspaper, *California Stylist* and *California Apparel News*, respectively, assumed a major role in promoting the market whose advertising dollars supported their effort. The journals held "Fashion Fiestas" in Palm Springs, which attracted buyers from all over America who hoped to combine work and vacation.

The buyers also made side trips from southern California to San Francisco, where

THE FASHIONISTS, active as a group from 1926 to 1960, had a common cause: communicate to buyers and the press that *the look of California was new*, and it suited the

a respectable fashion industry had grown up since the 1940s. One of the best-known labels was Koret of California, whose designer, Stephanie Koret, launched several fashion firsts such as permanently pleated cotton, and the use of a cotton fabric that was machine washable and machine dryable without wrinkles. She also introduced permanently creased pants and shorts, both styles that were made for more than sixty years. Nearby, Adolph Schumann was the colorful owner of Lilli Ann, a maker of extremely flamboyant suits, coats, and evening dresses. Although he advertised in high-fashion magazines, his Hollywood-inspired suits were favorites in San Francisco red-light districts. He was also the first California manufacturer to open a boutique in Paris. Koret and Schumann led the way for Jessica McClintock, Jane Tise, Doug and Susie Tompkins of the Plain Jane Dress Co. (who changed the name to Esprit de Corps, which remains a staple in department stores as Esprit), the Gap, and Banana Republic. The early San Francisco manufacturers and designers made their town a must-stop on buyers' trips west.

After the war, the fashion industry was able to show Hollywood a few things about hype. Fashion as theater emerged. Major movie studios did cross-promotions, providing personal appearances of stars of such magnitude as Cary Grant and Rosalind Rus-

FAIR JOYCE SHOES, shown with Rudi Gernreich sportswear, worn by Jimmy Mitchell in 1954.

sell. (These events lasted well into the 1960s when the likes of Mary Tyler Moore and Dick Van Dyke would meet and greet the retailers and editors.) By 1946 the outings had gone over the top, and budgets had no limits. A Los Angeles fabric company got in on the act and chartered a train to take the press, designers, and manufacturers from Los Angeles to the Grand Canyon. In a bit of unplanned drama, Hollywood's famed photographer John Engstead was shooting designer Dede Johnson against the backdrop of the Canyon on a balustrade of Bright Angel Lodge. The designer lost her balance and tumbled backward into the vast abyss. As she fell, disappearing from sight, she grasped a bush that was growing several yards down, and there she clung until national park rangers were lowered down to save her. For Johnson, even the huge amount of press coverage wasn't worth the near-death experience.

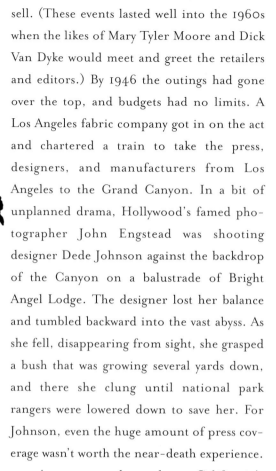

At events such as these, California's unique take on fashion was showcased. Sometimes the focus would be on a single item, such as the year Juli Lynne Charlot, a costume designer, made a circular skirt of felt. Although the first featured Christmas baubles, it was the "poodle" skirt with its appliqués of the French canine complete with collar and leash that became the stuff of news. The *poodle* became a classic symbol of the 1950s, copied worldwide.

JULI LYNNE CHARLOT decorated felt skirts with imaginative appliqués and created coordinated tops. Her danceable, whirlable skirts became a great hit with bobby-soxers, such as her '50s felt "poodle skirt."

ANNETTE FUNICELLO MODELS her poodle skirt.

Sportswear designers took a cue from the loose "chemise" silhouette that was emanating from Paris and kept the fit of separates nice and easy. In that spirit, Irene Kasmer, designer for Ardee Sportswear, dropped the waistline of her skirts and pants to rest on the hipbones—"Hip-Huggers," she called them. Kasmer says that she registered the design and name in 1958.

Throughout the latter half of the twentieth century, California's fashion industry continued to promote its wares through various promotional organizations. In 1976 a savvy group of young designers teamed to call themselves "contemporary" manufacturers (a term used to capture the essence of Baby Boomer women before the "boomer" term had been coined). Staging a fashion show at the Pacific Design Center (or Blue Whale, as the Cesar Pelli–designed blue glass building was called), the show featured the designs of Rudi Gernreich, Holly Harp, Harriet Selwyn, Phyllis Sues, Norma Fink, Nancy Heller, Barbara Dulin, Christine Albers, Dennis Goldsmith, and Irene Tsu. A huge success with more than a thousand retailers in attendance, the show earned *Vogue* magazine coverage that recognized "the new wave from California."

As Alice Hughes, a King Features writer, noted as far back as 1955, California designers "excel in the three P's: Pool, Patio and moving Picture modes. Why shouldn't they?

These are the clothes they need for the life they lead: swimming and sunning. They're *sexy*, young, DARING, or modest; they stretch so that one suit can fit six sizes, and they give a woman a bon-bon look. Could one ask for more?"

# HOORAY FOR

## *Old Hollywood*

GARBO VAMPS HER way through *Mata Hari* (1931) in the fabulous wardrobe—including this slinky gold lamé outfit—designed by the great Hollywood costumer Adrian.

WHEN NEW YORKER Jesse Lasky sent his best friend, Cecil B. DeMille, to Hollywood to scout locations for a studio and a new movie, fashion was the last thing on his mind. By 1916, when Lasky, his brother-in-law Samuel Goldfish (who would later change his name to Goldwyn), DeMille, and another movie maker named Adolph Zukor merged their businesses to form the most important motion picture studio in Hollywood, Famous Players–Lasky, they still had no idea that ultimately the clothes they put on their stars' backs would help bring people to the movies for the remainder of the century.

In eleven short years Famous Players–Lasky had changed its name to Paramount, and by then Gloria Swanson, Pola Negri, and Clara Bow had taught the male executives a thing or two about fashion—glamorous fashion, that is. These women, who had starred in silent films for Famous Players–Lasky, were starting trends that were sweeping the country. And although Swanson had become a star partially because she had a large personal wardrobe that helped save dollars on costume budgets, stars and their fans were demanding more extravagant costumes, costumes that evoked everything that sparkled about Hollywood.

It was to a glamour-hungry Hollywood that Howard Greer came in 1923, when he

In 1926 GREER left Paramount to open his own salon. Otto Olsen's Klieglights opened in 1927 on Sunset Boulevard. It featured a doorman, a circular stairway, and a desk with a guestbook. Greer, primarily known as a cocktail dress designer, let it be known that his dresses "showed over the table." He made up names for all his models (Barbara Marx—later Mrs. Frank Sinatra—was one of them). But it was the names he gave his clothes that so amused his clients, rich or famous, and the press.

*at*

j w Robinson co

*california*

was named the first official head costume designer at Famous Play-ers–Lasky. His first challenge was to create an image for Negri. He writes in his book, *Designing Male*, about work-ing on a Negri film:

". . . [T]he sky was the limit and we would shoot the works. The bank clerk's little helpmeet greeted her guests in a shimmering silver sheath, solidly embroidered in rhinestones and pearls. She wore twenty ropes of pearls and carried a fan of aigrettes. When the picture was released, the exhibitors shouted their approval, the public

*howard greer*

wrote letters of love, and Mr. Lasky gave me his personal accolade and a raise in salary. Into this carnivalesque atmosphere I was plummeted. There I wallowed in rhinestones and feathers and furs and loved every minute of it. And I was getting along famously with Pola."

Dressing Negri and Bow, Greer was busy full time and needed an assistant to help with all these excesses. In answer to Greer's ad for a sketch artist, a young art student with a "face like a pussycat" applied with a portfolio of sketches that immediately qualified her for the job, in the lead designer's estimation. Only after he hired her did Edith Head admit that she had "borrowed" the drawings from her fellow students.

Greer, who had set the glamorous tone for the studio, left Famous Players–Lasky before it became Paramount and went on to be a custom designer with his own salon and a long list of stars who were loyal to his talent. He later expanded into ready-to-wear with beautiful designs that were outrageously named: *"Tits on a half shell," "Ass in a sling," "Blind nuns underwater,"* and *"Whoops, got her!"*

Greer was replaced at Famous Players–Lasky by Travis Banton, who had designed for the New York fashion house Madame Frances and had created the wedding dress Mary Pickford wore when she married Douglas Fairbanks. With that credential alone, he was Hollywood ready.

By the time Banton arrived, the studio system had taken over in the film industry. With stars under contract to a motion-picture production organization, the studios strictly controlled the careers of their actors and actresses. Using powerful public relations departments and costume design departments with lavish budgets, film moguls determined not only what roles they played but where the stars lived and in what kinds of homes, what cars they drove, how and where they appeared in public, whom they dated, and of course, what they wore. *A star had to be dressed like a star at all times.* And it was up to studio costume designers to make certain that the celebrities had exactly the right clothes to wear, both on-screen and off.

Banton's talent was so remarkable
that in the twenty-first century his name
remains on the list of the world's most
influential fashion designers, a man
whose work dominated the screen
throughout the 1930s. His muse
was Marlene Dietrich, who, as
legendary fashion historian

Mae Diana Vreeland noted, West

"was a fat *hausfrau* on arrival
in Hollywood"—and then she
met Banton. "Banton made Dietrich," Vreeland extolled. He found ways
to highlight her legs, whether by baring
them as he did in *Blue Angel*, or covering them
as he did in her offscreen, man-tailored
suits. She became a svelte symbol of style
around the world, thanks to the designer's
creativity. He can single-handedly take
credit for dressing a woman like a man
and making it work. Banton also col-
laborated with Mae West to create
her voluptuous image, playing
up the curves of her hourglass
figure rather than straight-
ening them out as the
style of the day dictat-
ed. Her oversized
hats, plethora of
diamonds, feathers,
and lace were a holdover
from the Gay '90s barroom
girls, a look she clung to even as
flapper fashion got sleek. While
her glamour was a study in nostalgia,
it was drenched in sex appeal, something
that censors abhorred and the public craved.

As the studio system tightened its grip on its stars, and this Hollywood breed of glamour became essential to new films, costume designers necessarily became integral to each film. Every studio hired a staff of designers to dress its stable of stars. As early as the mid-1920s, stars began writing fashion demands into their contracts. Clotheshorses Mae West and Marlene Dietrich wanted real furs, imported laces, hand-embroideries, and fine workmanship in their wardrobes. They also wanted to be certain that they owned the gowns of their choice, an early industry perk that stuck for decades.

By the time Edith Head took over Paramount's wardrobe department in 1938, replacing Banton, whose career ended because of his alcoholism, she had fine-tuned everything she had learned, first from Greer and then from Banton. She continued dressing Paramount's stars—West, Dietrich, Swanson, Claudette Colbert, and Carole Lombard—but built her reputation when she created Dorothy Lamour's sarong for the film *Jungle Princess*, a style Lamour went on to wear in numerous films, including several of the *Road* films she made with Bing Crosby and Bob Hope.

At the helm of Paramount's wardrobe department in its heyday, Head was in charge of dressing every important star who graced the studio's cast list and many who worked for other studios if they requested her: Barbara Stanwyck, Ingrid Bergman, Bette Davis, Elizabeth Taylor, Grace Kelly, Audrey Hepburn. But she also spent a great deal of her time promoting film fashion. In the 1940s she saw to it that movie magazines were filled with fashion photographs from her newest films (a promotional move that other studios quickly adopted), thus making style an important aspect of every movie. These photographs were taken by the studio photographers, many of whom have come to be counted among the finest portrait talents in history: George Hurrell, John Engstead, Ray Jones, and Clarence Bull. These were the men who knew

how to work with light and makeup artists (think Max Factor and the renowned Westmore brothers) and costume designers to translate the concept of glamour in all its glory and create a longing for it in the public's imagination.

Shrewd enough to know that if glamour and fashion were a must, so too was her talent, Head ensured the jobs of costume designers by leading the move to establish the first Academy Awards for fashion design in color and black-and-white films in 1948. Although she didn't win that first Oscar, she went on to win eight, a record for costume design still unbroken at the beginning of the twenty-first century, and one that will most likely never be challenged: the job of studio designer met its demise in the 1960s, thus limiting the number of films any independent designer is likely to do.

While Banton and Head were busily making movie costumes at Paramount in the 1930s, designer Gilbert Adrian was creating the most-talked-about gowns in the world—it just happened that they too were used in films. Adrian, who headed the costume department at MGM, studied couture fashion design in Paris until he was discovered by Irving Berlin and asked to return to New York to create costumes for the Music Box Review. He was there discovered by Natasha Rambova, the wife of matinee idol Rudolph Valentino, who

whisked him off to Hollywood. En route, Adrian suffered through the idiosyncracies of the Valentinos and their considerable entourage, including sharing his berth with their pet monkey, who had taken a shine to the designer. But the trip was worth it. After working briefly at Paramount, where Valentino starred, Adrian went to MGM with Cecil B. DeMille when the director defected to the rival studio in 1929.

Louis B. Mayer gave Adrian a contract as head designer immediately. Adrian's work was featured in the lavish, big-budget productions created by MGM's famed production designer, Irving Thalberg. Adrian's biggest film, *Marie Antoinette*, starring Norma Shearer (Thalberg's wife), required four thousand costumes, five years of research, and trips to Europe to buy silks and brocades. As one Hollywood gossip columnist of the day noted, "Because his clothes are worn by the biggest stars in the biggest pictures, he has more influence on women's clothes than any man in history."

Indeed, movies had become the voice of fashion. Magazines such as *Vogue* and *Harper's Bazaar* took a backseat to the likes of *Photoplay* and *Movie Mirror*. Women wanted to dress like their favorite movie stars and copied the fashions of their movies. The styles created by California costume designers were shaping the trends of the country.

This ADRIAN DRESS worn by Joan Crawford in *Letty Lynton* (1932) was copied by manufacturers.

ADRIAN DID ALL his own sketches, sometimes working on four films at a time. His talent extended beyond his workroom: he loved to paint and collect antiques (he had his own shop), and he designed home interiors for his friends.

*Opposite:* GILBERT ADRIAN, NÉ Adolph Greenberg, with one of his favorite stars, Greta Garbo.

No style had more impact in the 1940s than the broad-shouldered look Adrian created for Joan Crawford. Created as a means to draw attention away from her relatively thick waist and wide hips, Crawford's football-shouldered suits and dresses swept the country.

Adrian's simple, clean-lined ensembles for Greta Garbo and the slinky, bias-cut gowns for Jean Harlow were copied in all price categories at the retail level and showed up in store windows almost as quickly as they appeared on the screen. The Sears Roebuck catalogue featured endorsements by stars to help sell the clothes. Whether it was little Shirley Temple or stylish Joan Crawford, clothes with "autographed labels" became status symbols. Even for the woman who could only afford to pay $1.98 for a felt fedora, Ginger Rogers's embroidered "signature" on a label made the hat far more desirable than the unsigned $1 version.

Adrian left MGM to open his own couture salon after receiving terrible reviews for his work in the last film of Greta Garbo, his muse. Studio executives had forced him to stray from the slim, unadorned silhouettes that had become the star's signature in favor of more extravagant, heavily embellished gowns—and the results were disastrous.

Adrian was replaced by Irene Gibbons. In the 1940s Irene dressed Dietrich, Katharine Hepburn, Ginger Rogers, Greer

ADRIAN'S POST-HOLLYWOOD collection retained the padded-shoulder suits he first created for Joan Crawford.

*Opposite left*: RENIE CONLEY'S WHITE-COLLARED dress, designed for Ginger Rogers in the film *Kitty Foyle*, became a popular knock-off made by manufacturers.

*Opposite right*: DOROTHY JEAKINS WON the first Oscar presented for costume design in color in 1948, for *Joan of Arc*, starring Ingrid Bergman.

Garson, Ingrid Bergman, and Rosalind Russell. Frustrated by the pace and politics of studio design, Irene too left Hollywood to design for private customers. After viewing one of Irene's couture fashion shows, her friend and competitor Howard Greer stated that "coming from seeing my show, it was like going from a whorehouse to a cathedral." Irene's elegance extended from the hushed magnificence of her suits and day dresses to the suble but grand sweep of her evening gowns, all shown on willowy models who reflected the quiet of her showroom.

Numerous other costumers gained fame as their names appeared on the screen and their designs appeared in retail stores all over America. Jean Louis created two of the most talked-about gowns in Hollywood history: the black gown made famous by Rita Hayworth in *Gilda* and the dress worn by Marilyn Monroe when she sang "Happy Birthday" to President John F. Kennedy at Madison Square Garden—auctioned off at Christie's in 1999 for $1.26 million.

Walter Plunkett designed the costumes for *Gone With The Wind* (1939), garments that were often called the best researched in the history of film costume. Renie Conley took the spotlight at RKO with her designs for Ginger Rogers in *Kitty Foyle*. Knock-offs of her white-collared dress became a hit on Seventh Avenue.

Dorothy Jeakins won the first Academy

Award for costume design in color in 1948 for *Joan of Arc*, the same year that Roger F. Furse was honored for his work in the black-and-white film *Hamlet*. Contemporary (rather than historical) costumes did not receive an award in films until 1950, when Edith Head won the Oscar for *All About Eve*. The film's signature off-the-shoulder gown worn by Bette Davis, however, was actually a mistake of poor fitting: "It was too big for her, but it was too late to re-fit the gown," Head admitted. "So Bette just pulled it off her shoulders and went to the set." The dress was copied by ready-to-wear manufacturers for retail stores.

Juel Park knew stars intimately. The Hollywood designer worked in bias-cut, transparent silks to create glamorous, sensual underwear and negligees, bringing new sexiness to old-fashioned nightgowns. Juel's sister, Sue, an art student, would sketch Juel's design and top it with a star's face. Many of her fur and maribou-trimmed styles are still copied today.

Helen Rose, head costumer at MGM for more than twenty years, designed the wedding dress that Grace Kelly wore when she married Prince Rainier of Monaco in 1956. Copies of the gown became the runaway favorite for brides-to-be for the next two years.

Orry-Kelly became Bette Davis's main designer, but his work for Ingrid Bergman in *Casablanca* and Marilyn Monroe in *Some Like It*

Carole Lombard

Helen Rose was the costumer at MGM for more than twenty years and won two Oscars. She designed Elizabeth Taylor's wardrobe for *Cat on a Hot Tin Roof* (1958). Her pièce de résistance, however, was the gown she designed for the wedding of Grace Kelly to Prince Rainier in 1956. It was *the* wedding dress, and many brides wanted dresses just like it.

*Hot* created retail trends throughout the United States. The Australian received his first Hollywood job through his friend Cary Grant. Although his styles for Rosalind Russell in *Auntie Mame* were too outrageous for copies, many people later credited Orry-Kelly's work on the film with freeing the American woman to wear vibrant colors and bold prints.

Elois Jenssen, who shared an Oscar for her work in Cecil B. DeMille's *Samson and Delilah*, was a pioneer in another important field: costume design for television. Her

wardrobe for **Lucille Ball in** *I Love Lucy* **influenced fashion in the 1950s—** Ball played a housewife who dressed in adaptations of Christian Dior's postwar "New Look."

Hollywood glamour has been in demand from the earliest days of film. During the Golden Age of movies, stars under contract to studios were more important than any fashion models. The talented people in the design rooms of California studios shaped the fashions and then let film stars communicate those California inspirations and interpretations to the rest of the world.

*Opposite:* CALIFORNIAN ELOIS JENSSEN was the original costume designer of *I Love Lucy* (1953–55 seasons). Lucille Ball's look was a tremendous fashion influence in the 1950s.

THIS FAMOUS PINUP of Rita Hayworth in a seductive, black lace–trimmed nightie, posed on an unmade bed, was photographed by Bob Landry for *Life* magazine in 1941. But rather than a studio designer, it was Columbia's publicist, Maggie Maskel, who created the sexy slip.

6

# THE GOLDEN *boys*

The Golden Boys of the '50s (and two women): Bill Pearson, unidentified woman, Bud Kilpatrick, Rudi Gernreich, Dan Werle, William Travilla, Helen Rose, Gus Tassell, Paul Whitney, and Jimmy Galanos. Photograph by Gordon Parks for *Life* magazine, 1959.

By 1950 CALIFORNIA's reputation as the Mecca for innovative sportswear and swimwear as well as for extravagant Hollywood designer salons was clearly established. Young designers were thriving in these sun-friendly markets, and costume designers who had begun creating ensembles and gowns for the public were still drawing a sophisticated, wealthy clientele who might otherwise have spent their fashion dollars in Paris or, at least, New York. The onslaught of retailers coming to California from the East in the late 1940s had given California manufacturers the confidence to begin entering the dress-suit market, offering the suit departments of the country's specialty and department stores another **CALIFORNIA LOOK:** broad-shouldered suits, with defined waistlines and pushed-up or seven-eighths sleeves—*inspired by Adrian* but not priced like his couture designs. These relatively affordable ensembles became another dependable staple from California in the mid- to late 1950s.

But the same confidence that allowed designers such as Gene Shelley, Edith Small, and Charles Wilpan to tackle dressed-up suits at moderate prices led a new breed of designers to create high fashion—their own collections of daytime dresses and ensembles, cocktail fare, and evening gowns. A golden age of fashion was dawning in the Golden State,

and with it came a coterie of avant-garde male designers known as the "Golden Boys."

These Golden Boys—among them Don Loper, William Travilla, Gus Tassell, Dan Werle, Paul Whitney, Michael Novarese, Bud Kilpatrick, William Pearson, James Galanos, and Rudi Gernreich—offered relief from the tailored suit, but more important, they added diversity to the styles that were emanating from California. Their metier was a soft, feminine take on fashion. To remain apart from the uptight suits and the casual sportswear designs produced in the heart of Los Angeles's downtown garment center, these inspired designers opened their ateliers away from the fray—on Sunset Boulevard in West

WILLIAM TRAVILLA DESIGNED retail and costumes for numerous films in the '40s, '50s, and '60s, including gowns for Marilyn Monroe in *Gentlemen Prefer Blondes* (1953) and *The Seven Year Itch* (1955) (opposite).

# "*Have* SAMPLES, *will* TRAVEL."

Hollywood, in Beverly Hills, wherever the vibe was good and the rent was cheap. Urged on by fans, friends, and investors who were willing to put up the relatively small capital it took to start a fashion house in California, these dynamic individuals with their disparate backgrounds and divergent takes on style, created reputations for themselves and gave buyers another reason to head west.

The Golden Boys' unspoken motto was "Have samples, will travel." At an important buyer's request, they would board a plane, bagged samples slung over their arms, and head for an advertised personal appearance—a trunk show—anywhere in the country. While the designer hoped to take custom orders based on the new styles he carried in his "trunk," the store buyers were happy if the increased customer traffic in the store resulted in the sale of a scarf, hat, or handkerchief by those who couldn't afford designer fare. Well-heeled clientele reveled in the attention the designer provided and relished his means of translating a size-6 sample into a size-14 sale. In the buying frenzy that followed these in-store fashion presentations, the department personnel maintained sharp eyes, to be sure no two women in the same social circle ordered identical styles. Retailers made money and designers got publicity as fashion-starved women's editors from local news-

PAUL WHITNEY'S HALLMARK is a crisp, uncluttered line for daytime, with emphasis on glamorous evening clothes. Shown is his 1950s evening gown in silk chiffon and shantung.

DAVID HAYES'S RED silk evening pantsuit, spring 2000.

SPRING 1964

papers hurried to interview the visiting style dignitaries from California.

All of the Golden Boys gained fame for different reasons, but two of the men became fashion legends internationally. Both established their fashion signatures on the West Coast fashion scene in 1951, encouraged by the Hollywood costume designer Jean Louis, both were supported by retailers in Beverly Hills to follow their respective dreams, and both were elected to fashion's coveted Coty Hall of Fame, but the two men were as different as a California sunrise and sunset—Galanos designed for the elites and Gernreich for the beats.

# GALANOS

"I'm only interested in designing for a certain type of woman," Los Angeles designer James Galanos, one of the very few American couturiers, candidly admitted. "Specifically, one that has money. In addition, she must be tall, slim, and small boned—model sized." Having established his criteria, Galanos became a magnet for exactly the clientele he wanted, from Marlene Dietrich, Loretta Young, and Diana Ross to the woman for whom he coined the phrase "Reagan Red," Nancy Reagan.

Hollywood costumer Jean Louis gave Galanos his start in the specialty fashion business by lending him the capital and introducing him to a gifted dressmaker, Madame Marguerite, who had worked for Hattie Carnegie. Perhaps Jean Louis recognized more than just their similarities of artistic talent and fastidious attention to detail—like the famed costumer, Galanos was shy and unassuming, an impeccable dresser with manners that reflected an old-world charm.

After Galanos sold a dozen of his skill-fully crafted and artfully draped gowns to Saks Fifth Avenue in Beverly Hills, another Beverly Hills retailer, Amelia Gray, saw his remarkable talent and bought Galanos gowns for her prestigious shop, despite their sky-high price tags. She paid her bills on time and bought the Philadelphia-born designer's extraordinary gowns season after season. Because of her early support, Galanos returned the favor by giving her exclusive access to his collection in the Los Angeles area for many years. By 1952 he was ready to take his collection to New York, at first showing in a hotel room and the following year working from a friend's apartment.

He became known as master of the "little nothing" dress. The fabrics were the finest in the world—hand selected by Galanos in the most elite fabric mills of Europe—and "you could wear a dress inside out and no one would know, because it was so beautifully made," Nancy Reagan once said. But his beaded cocktail and evening dresses were also deceptively simple, encrusted with jewel-like beads that were distinctively Galanos style. He designed both of Nancy Reagan's Inaugural Ball gowns. His one-shouldered gown of re-

embroidered French chantilly lace sparked with a subtle sprinkling of crystals, beads, and rhinestones is displayed with other First Ladies' historic gowns in a gallery in the Smithsonian Institution, Washington, D.C.

Galanos dressed the world's elite women, while designers all over marveled at the quality of his work, especially because it was created in California. Hubert de Givenchy was quoted as saying, "We don't make them this well in Paris." This is the legacy Galanos left when he retired in 1998.

GALANOS IS BEST KNOWN for his cocktail and smocked chiffon evening dresses. A conservative designer, he shaped clothes that were complicated in structure—yet looked deceptively simple.

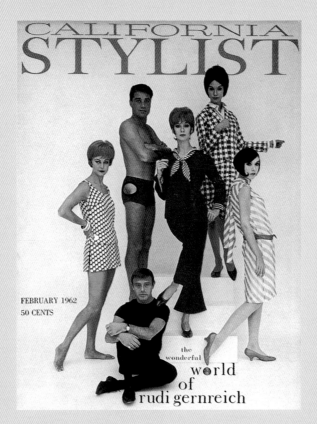

The cover of *California Stylist*, February 1961.

FEBRUARY 1962
50 CENTS

the wonderful world of rudi gernreich

## Rudi Gernreich

Perhaps fashion critic Cathy Horyn captured the essence of Rudi Gernreich when she wrote of him in *Vanity Fair* in 1998, twenty-three years after his death:

"Rudi Gernreich was the first bona fide fashion guru designer to come out of California's youth culture of the '60s . . . . No designer came close to evoking the era's new freedom or to ventilating high fashion with more pure fun! GERNREICH *was one of a kind,* a singular cross between Old World radical and space-age aesthete, with a dash of Barnum thrown in."

Designers such as Mary Quant and

Andre Courrèges were also at the forefront of the world's youth culture, but it was Gernreich's innovation that has had the longest lasting impact on the world of fashion, both intellectually and stylistically. For students of design, Gernreich will always be considered the futurist, the designer who started creating clothes for the year 2000 in 1964. His vision of the future included color, fun, sex, style, and freedom. His mission was to free a woman's body. He began his quest when he created the bra-free swimsuit, the knitted tube dress, the topless bathing suit, the no-bra bra, and the thong bikini, all styles that have been studied and restudied, defined and redefined, copied and usurped, but never mastered in the Gernreich way.

Born in Vienna in 1922, the young Rudi was inspired by his aunt's dress shop, where he spent hours drawing gowns. At the age of twelve, he was offered an apprenticeship by an Austrian designer. But rather than let him travel alone to London, where the designer would be working, his mother kept Rudi at home, close to her. Four years later, as anti-semitism worsened in Austria, he and his mother escaped to California. He attended Los Angeles City College, worked at RKO Studios in the publicity department, and even temporarily worked for Paramount designer Edith Head. But his interest at the time was not in designing costumes.

GERNREICH PATTERNED THIS dress after his swimsuits.

*Opposite:* LAUREN BACALL (shown with her son) wearing Rudi's tunic and skinny pants.

RUDI'S PINK-AND-ORANGE knit dress, worn by model Rosemarie Stack. Rudi designed the knit fabrics for all of his clothes.

RUDI'S GRAY-AND-WHITE check jacket (for Westwood Knitting Mills). Photographed by Christa for *Life* cover, 1954.

During a brief stint with a Los Angeles dance troupe, Gernreich supported himself by designing fabrics, where he discovered one of his true talents. From there he traveled to New York to design coats and suits, but he quickly returned to Los Angeles, stymied by the lack of courage and creativity he was exposed to on Seventh Avenue: "I was bursting with original ideas, but they were always rejected because they did not fit into the French idiom."

He returned to Los Angeles and eventually formed a partnership with Walter Bass, a sportswear manufacturer who discovered Gernreich's designs at a small Beverly Hills boutique called Matthews. His first collection for Bass featured flowing monastic dresses that were tightly belted with long string ties, in gingham and cotton tweed. The styles quickly landed in Jax, another Beverly Hills shop, and "in one hour everything was gone," Gernreich later recalled. Gernreich worked with Bass until 1959.

Peggy Moffitt was a salesgirl for Jax who became Gernreich's muse and model in the 1960s. Moffitt's husband, photographer William Claxton, captured Gernreich's avant-garde designs with Moffitt's body and face as canvas—and Gernriech's lasting image

was etched in fashion history. Few who study fashion will ever forget his topless swimsuit, a garment he designed specifically for the fashion editor of *Look* magazine, who wanted to show the bathing suit of the future. The 1964 magazine photo turned into one of the most important statements in fashion history, and it elevated Gernreich to the ranks of the world's most important designers. The bare suit—which he designed under his own label, G. R. Design, Inc.—would haunt the designer for years, always overshadowing the recognition of his real talent.

THE OPENING SCENE of the Rudi Gernreich retrospective show produced by the Los Angeles Fashion Group at Los Angeles's famed Wiltern Theater in 1986.

A master showman, Gernreich played the press like a fiddle. He knew what would get featured, but he often overlooked what would sell. When he decided twice that he was through with fashion design and made brief forays into the food world and into tabletop design, the fashion world was deprived of the thoughtful, witty, and charming attitude that marked the Rudi Gernreich style.

The Hell's Angels were hired to keep the peace at the weekly dances and love-ins.

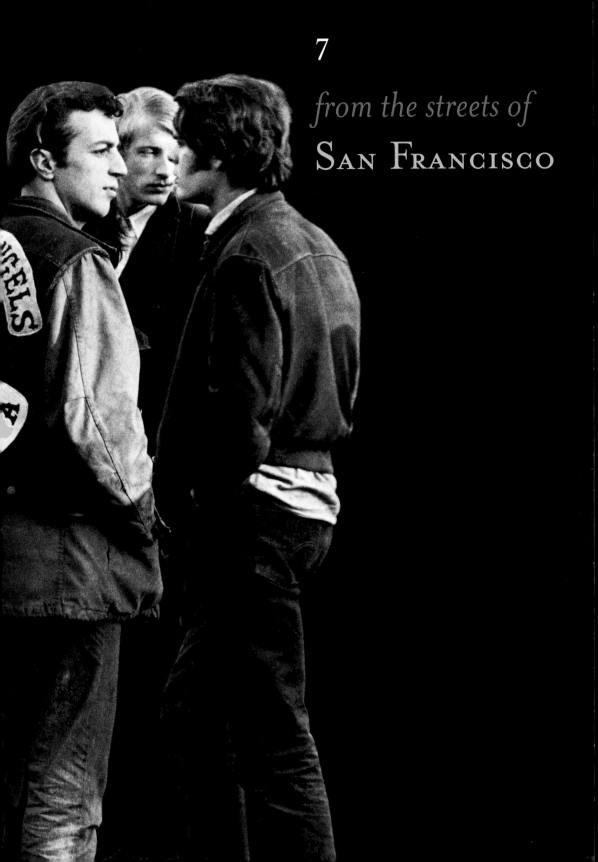

*from the streets of*

SAN FRANCISCO

ALTHOUGH THE WORD *psychedelic* was coined in 1956, the public wouldn't grasp its true meaning until the Love Generation was born in San Francisco in the early 1960s. Then the term defined not just a mindset but colors, art forms, music, and fashion. Spawned by the beat poets and writers who dug the coffee houses of San Francisco's North Beach in the 1950s, the hippie counter-culture filled the 1960s with sex, drugs, and rock 'n' roll. Marijuana had survived from the beat scene, but LSD was the singular division between aging beatniks and young hippies. The Age of Aquarius was born in an acid bath of color, passion, and design, elements that created the lasting fashion influence of the 1960s.

As Barney Hoskyn wrote in *Beneath the Diamond Sky* in 1997, "Clubs began opening up all over the Bay Area, luring restless middle class teens, privileged enough to do what no one had the luxury of doing before . . . to see through the hollowness of America's consumer society." Young men turned away from the khakis and plaid shirts of the 1950s teenagers and instead donned the tattered

A LOVE-IN, 1967.

*Opposite:* JOHN SEBASTIAN, of the band the Lovin' Spoonful, in psychedelic tie-dye.

*Opposite:* Flower power—with Twiggy eyelashes, 1968.

And a Love Fest, 1968.

A Fool fashion show featuring bagpipers at the Aquarius Theater in Hollywood. Fool, an artistic team of Marika and Simone from Holland, were hired to paint the old Earl Carroll Theater, transforming it to the Aquarius for the production of *Hair*.

jeans of the working class and the fringed suedes of the Native American. Young women opened up trunks to find the long dresses granny had worn, or they stitched up Victorian-looking velvet-and-lace robes that spoke of another era. If the young were to truly reject a consumer society, handcrafts and artistry were the way to personalize these hand-me-down looks. Batiks, airbrushed, and tie-dye patterns became signatures not just of a fashion but of a social and political movement.

Musicians were among the first to popularize the hippie look, adapting it from the streets of San Francisco—universally referred to as Haight-Ashbury despite the fact that hippies dwelled all over the City by the Bay, beyond the confines of the famed corner. Groups with names like the Jefferson Airplane, the Grateful Dead, the Family Dog, the Charlatans, and Big Brother and the Holding Company played to the stages of America, communicating the dressed-down trend that was quickly sweeping America. Janis Joplin and Grace Slick, the queens of the San Francisco scene, were featured in the pages of fashion magazines, and New York's Broadway gave San Francisco style its nod of approval with the stage production of *Hair*, billed as a tribal-rock musical and one of the longest-running productions of the 1960s.

Retailers, designers, and manufacturers recognized the commercial potential of the

# JEFFERSON AIRPLANE

## SUN. NOV. 6TH

FILLMORE AUDITORIUM 9-2 AM FILLMORE-GEARY SAN FRANCISCO

HAIR, a smash success "American tribal love rock musical," debuted in New York and then toured the country. But by that time, the San Francisco scene had cooled down. Woodstock, in August 1969, and the Bay Area concert, at the Altamont Speedway in December, were the last rock festivals of that legendary era. But the fashion influence hovered like a drug-induced haze.

looks on the streets. Used-clothing stores and leather crafters, such as North Beach Leathers, whose clothing became a staple for rich hippies around the world, thrived. Designers such as Linda Gravenites, who fashioned clothes for Joplin, and Jessica McClintock, who started selling granny dresses in a San Francisco boutique called Gunne Sax, became high-powered fashion gurus, catering to a different strata of the hippie world.

By the late 1960s even the Beatles had given up the Mod London look of Mary Quant and now dressed in love beads and embroidered shirts. They traded their clean-cut mop-tops for straggly long hair and their

*Opposite:* THE NEW YORK hippie scene was reenacted in the 1979 film version of the '60s musical *Hair.*

clean-shaven faces for mustachioed, bearded ones. Paris caught the hippie bug too, with designers such as Yves St. Laurent, Marc Bohan of Dior, Ungaro, Hubert de Givenchy, and even the staid Madame Grès keying into gypsy, hippie, Bohemian, and Indian looks. In New York, Oscar de la Renta, Halston, Giorgio Sant' Angelo, Betsey Johnson, and Stephen Burrows were inspired by the same styles.

In Los Angeles, designers who catered to the Hollywood set adapted hippie looks as well. Holly Harp created diaphanous silk gowns with rippling "lettuce" edges, styles that became synonymous with the Hollywood hipster girls, both on-screen and off. Bob Mackie

The Charlatans, a blues-and-country folk band who wore thrift-store, dandy, Edwardian, Western finery, formed in 1965 in San Francisco.

established himself at the center of hippie hipdom, when his mind-expanding costumes helped turned rock 'n' roll singer Cher into a fashion legend.

Indeed, as the twentieth century turned, Cher was honored at the eighteenth annual American Fashion Awards given by the Council of Fashion Designers of America in New York, recognized for her long impact on style. She has always remained true to her hippie roots, challenging the styles of the day and offering her own counterculture interpretation. But not just Cher resurfaced as the lasting icon of the love generation. So too did

the styles of Haight-Ashbury and the music that defined Woodstock. What was originally a street look has since been adopted by expensive labels. Gucci introduced peasant blouses and beaded jeans, while Dior, Gaultier, Fendi, Dolce & Gabbana, and Versace have brought back the thrift-store look at high prices.

If there was one lasting fashion statement created on the streets of California, it was the T-shirt and jeans that hippies wore first in San Francisco and then throughout the world. No single look has been adopted and adapted more successfully. The T-shirt was first popularized in the 1950s by Marlon Brando in *Streetcar Named Desire* and *The Wild Ones*, but in the 1960s it became a billboard of sorts, broadcasting messages of love or anger. From those days in the mid–twentieth century to the present, the T-shirt has continued to be a form of communication that covers the body. It continues to speak as personal, political, or promotional statement.

The couture hippie style of Christian Dior, featured in *Vogue*, 1969.

*Opposite:* Xoxo illustrates the glamorous contemporary hippie look in chiffon and silk.

## 8
# EVERYBODY'S
# *Gone Surfing . . .*

TWO SURFERS WEARING SUITS by Roxy, owned by Quiksilver, the largest surfwear company.

IN 1907, WHEN twenty-three-year-old surfing champion George Freeth met railroad industrialist Henry E. Huntington, nobody envisioned that the world would be "surfing" cyberspace by the turn of the next century. Leave it to California to create the term.

Huntington hired Freeth to give demonstrations of this Hawaii-born water sport as a promotion for his new Los Angeles-to-Redondo Beach train line. Freeth's visit coincided with an article written by Jack London, who had just gotten hooked on surfing while in Hawaii. A few years later, when Waikiki beach boy Duke Kahanamoku won the 100-meter freestyle gold medal at the 1912 Olympics in Stockholm—and then admitted that his *real* passion was surfing—the world took notice of the sport. Tom Blake, a Wisconsin boy who fell in love with surfing, designed the first hollow surfboard in Hawaii in 1926, then moved to southern California, where he worked with Thomas N. Rogers of Venice, California, to manufacture it. California devotees turned surfing into a southern California sport. They found the perfect waves on the coast and set the stage for one of the biggest fashion trends to rock the world.

With their bleached blond hair and their *huarache* sandals from Mexico, 1950s surfers had their own well-defined look, whether out of the water in rolled-up Levi's or in the

FROM HOMEMADE BOARD shorts to high technology, the surf industry today, centered in Orange County, California, has expanded into a more than $2 billion giant—worldwide, year-round, for men, women, and children.

water in classic, tailored swim trunks. The trunks were structured like trousers, but hemmed at the thigh, tight through the hip, and not too quick to dry. If surfers wanted trunks that would allow more freedom of movement, they were dependent on the "surfer moms" or cotton-shop seamstresses up and down the coast from Malibu to San Clemente to stitch up pairs of trunks that were suitable for the sport.

In the early 1950s, inspired by surfing trips to Hawaii, California surfer and fabric producer Walter Hoffman and his brother Phil began producing Hawaiian-print shirts, something that could easily be worn with those not very comfortable, but available, trunks. Just a few years later, a Santa Cruz surfer named Jack O'Neill pioneered the wetsuit, using laminated neoprene and elastic nylon jersey, making it possible to surf year-round. "IT'S ALWAYS SUMMER *on the inside!*" was the slogan of O'Neill's suits, wave-worthy garb that helped bring surfing to a broader market.

In the summer of 1959—just after the foam board developed in 1958 by surfers Hobie Alter and Gordon Clark in Laguna Beach and the shortboard which followed in 1966 made surfing easier and more accessible—surfer Duke Boyd and seamstress Doris Moore whipped up a pair of wide-leg canvas shorts with a button-fly sewn in Dacron

thread. With that, Boyd and Moore founded Hang Ten (named in honor of the boarders' technique of extending ten toes over the nose of the surfboard). Then came Hang Ten's first lightweight nylon trunks, followed by the innovative use of Velcro on the fly and pockets. By 1971 Hang Ten had $18 million dollars in sales. The surf industry was on its way.

Surfing, music, girls, and cars at surf spot, San Onofre in Orange County, south of San Clemente, in 1948.

surfin' safari
THE BEACH BOYS
SURFIN' SAFARI ◆ 409 ◆ SURFIN' ◆ SUMMERTIME BLUES ◆ COUNTY FAIR
HEADS YOU WIN - TAILS I LOSE ◆ CUCKOO CLOCK ◆ MOON DAWG
THE SHIFT ◆ TEN LITTLE INDIANS ◆ CHUG-A-LUG ◆ LITTLE MISS AMERICA

Another California surfer, following his dream and living in Hawaii, was inspired by a *Life* magazine cover of Russians at the beach in their pajamas. Dave Rochlen urged his wife to make him a pair of laid-back pants he could board in. Rochlen wanted bottoms that felt like pajamas (no fly, drawstring waist, and abbreviated at the knee): he dubbed them "jams," and Surfline Hawaii was born. Fashioned in vivid Hawaiian prints, sold in California surf shops, they became the "in" style of the California surfer. Jams were photographed on Rochlen and a coterie of beach friends in a fashion section of *Life* magazine in 1965. Jim Jenks founded Ocean Pacific (OP) in the early 1970s, inventing the utilitarian double-stitched board shorts and corduroy shorts. Another new wave was about to peak.

At the same time that these clever surfer's were turning their hobby into clothing dollars, other newcomers to surfdom such as Dick Dale were picking up Fender guitars and making riffs that conjured images of riding a wave. He and his Del-Tones became the kings of the surf stomp (which replaced the sock hop). Then came the Beach Boys. *Surfin' Safari*, the Beach Boys' hit album of 1963, got the message across plainly and simply: *"Everybody's gone surfing, surfing USA."* Their surf sound and lyrics about riding waves, surf city, the sand, and California girls made it possible to transport the beach to places where the tide never ebbs.

Suddenly surf music was the biggest wave in the country.

And in the movie world, in 1959 sexy Sandra Dee starred as Gidget, a surfer girl whose character was based on the real life of beach bunny Kathy, the daughter of Malibu-based author Frederick Kohner. (The movie also gave real-life surfer Cliff Robertson the chance to become a star.) Movies were far from immune to trends. Propelled by the film's success, Hollywood spent the next decade making surf films—big moneymakers such as *Beach Party* (1963), which featured "seven new surfing hits" in addition to Frankie Avalon and Annette Funicello, *How to Stuff a Wild Bikini* (1965), and *Beach Blanket Bingo* (1965). Even Stevie Wonder's singing career was jump-started by *Muscle Beach Party* (1964).

Surfing was established as the California dream come true for America. After surfer John Severson founded *Surfer* magazine in 1959, more than thirty-five publications dedicated to board sports followed. True cult films such as Severson's *Big Wednesday* (1961) and Bruce Brown's *Endless Summer* (1966) showed the exhilaration of surfing that only true surfers could capture for the screen. The blend of Hollywood films and true surf chronicles provided something for every-one—zeitgeist surfers and hodaddies.

Awash in the 1970s as the British inva-sion took over in music and clothes, surfing

149

wear made a strong comeback in the 1980s as surfing and skateboarding found a new generation. Brands such as Stussy, Quiksilver, and Gotcha emerged out of nowhere—although Orange County was definitely "somewhere" to surfers. Quiksilver, founded by Bob McKnight and Jeff Hakman, both surfers, became the largest surfwear company in the world and the first to go public. More surf clothes companies emerged: No Fear, Body Glove, Billabong USA, Rusty. And their market seemed to just keep growing. By 1997 the United States had more than two million surfers . . . and multitudes of wannabes.

Soon lifestyle labels such as New York's Ralph Lauren and Tommy Hilfiger were dandifying the clothes that started in the sand. Lauren himself rented the entire Santa Bar-

BILLABONG CATERS to the girl surfers. Shown here, Billabong girls in surf casual Trance Tank and "Lotus" pants.

# The Endless Summer

bara Surf Museum in 1995 to use its collection in his New York showroom. And Hilfiger, according to the *Los Angeles Times* business section, waded "into surf wear niche market with insiders' help" when he turned to the Paskowitz family, a clan of nine children and their parents who lived in a bus, in constant search of the perfect wave. The clan had established a surfing camp in Orange County, a place where they could live and still surf. Hilfiger sponsored the Paskowitz Summer Surf Camp in San Onofre State Park, and the Paskowitz family lent its name and camp logo for Hilfiger T-shirts and caps.

Modern-day surf manufacturers target label-savvy kids who want to be associated with extreme sports. In merchandising terms, this is called "growing the customer." *Surfing* is

BRUCE BROWN's 1966 film *The Endless Summer* gave surfing national exposure and sent surf disciples around the world. To quote *Surfer Magazine*, "Bruce Brown distilled the grail quest to its purest form—the search for the perfect wave."

the granddaddy of board-oriented sports, including *skateboarding, snowboarding, wake boarding, wind surfing* (invented by Malibu surfers Hoyle Schweitzer and Jim Drake in 1960), and *kite surfing.* Together, these sports add up to year-round sales all over the world.

It is a long ride from the beach at Redondo in 1907 to surfing the web in the year 2000, but it is a direct one. The California dream instilled freedom in the minds of Americans who couldn't take to the water. Surfing is a freedom of the mind and spirit, a freedom born in California.

Roxy girls in the popular board shorts.

*Opposite: A skateboarder demonstrates his skills. Tony Hawk, the world champion skateboarder's company, is a division of Quiksilver.

9

## *The New* HOLLYWOOD

As the twenty-first century begins, the impact of California style emanates from one source: Hollywood—not the town but the industry. Whether the Hollywood fashion concept is communicated via television, film, or music, the message is clear and overpowering. But who controls it? Who is the fashion power behind the style from California?

Credit the stylist. Unlike the costume designer who styled a made-to-order image for each actor or actress, the stylist serves as a liaison between a fashion-conscious star and the fashion industry. The stylist was born of necessity. When the major studios gave up their control over the stars and their images in the early 1960s, actors and actresses attempted to take charge, a time-consuming endeavor that often failed. At first it made sense that Streisand would go shopping at offbeat boutiques in Beverly Hills to put together her wardrobe for *The Way We Were* or that Cher would haunt the Right Bank Shoe Company for a dozen pairs of perfect boots to wear in her off-camera hours. But it became clear that these experts of the screen weren't necessarily experts in style. Indeed, Mr. Blackwell's "Worst-Dressed List" emerged to attest to the fact. In addition, starstruck fans took to the stores in search of their favorite celebrities. Gone were stars' days of freedom when Jodie Foster could go suit shopping at Armani for herself, or Britney

In the music video for her 1985 song "Material Girl," Madonna drew inspiration from the William Travilla gown worn by Marilyn Monroe for the number "Diamonds Are a Girl's Best Friend," in *Gentlemen Prefer Blondes.*

Spears could pick out her own jeans. *A new category of Hollywood celebrity was born—* a celebrity known only to stars and to shop- keepers: a shopper who shops for the stars, the stylist. Stylists provide not just a shopping service, relieving celebrities from trying to find time to shop, but, more impor- tant, the best of them provide a consistent taste level that gives the star the look he or she wants. If slurs from the press begin to emerge, or the star tires of the stylist's inter- pretation of the star's look, the guillotine falls and another stylist takes over.

These professional shoppers select the handbag for the newest television sitcom star and bring a slew of gowns to the latest Oscar contender's home to help her make decisions about what to wear. They are the behind-the- scenes people who get paid by their stars and, often under the table, by the designers of apparel and accessories, to make a look hap- pen. Most of these modern-day Hollywood stylemakers live in California. If they select a Christian Lacroix ensemble, Gucci jeans, or a Versace gown for Gwyneth Paltrow, Jennifer Lopez, or Julia Roberts, they nevertheless style it with a West Coast flair. European elements simply become a part of the California look.

For a fashion designer, a gown seen on the Oscar stage represents a guaranteed increase in prestige and sales. During the pre-Oscar period, frenzy hits European fash-

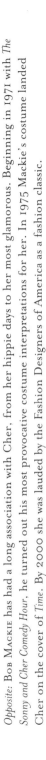

BOB MACKIE DESIGNED for The *Carol Burnett Show* for more than eleven years. Burnett has repeatedly said, "The key to Bob's success is that he has a producer's mind. His true genius lies in his zeal for detail and his sense of humor."

*Opposite:* BOB MACKIE has had a long association with Cher, from her hippie days to her most glamorous. Beginning in 1971 with *The Sonny and Cher Comedy Hour,* he turned out his most provocative costume interpretations for her. In 1975 Mackie's costume landed Cher on the cover of *Time.* By 2000 she was lauded by the Fashion Designers of America as a fashion classic.

RICHARD TYLER IS one of today's top California designers.

ion houses, Seventh Avenue design groups, and Los Angeles's hottest couturiers as they attempt to contact celebrities, via their stylists, offering the opportunity to receive complimentary gowns. An actress might receive offers of dozens of gowns—all she had to do was select one to wear to the Academy Awards, spread the *name of its designer,* **AND IT WAS HERS FOR KEEPS.** Not a bad trade-off, but such offers have become fraught with politics and competition, and the gowns no longer have the cachet they once had.

The jewelry celebrities wear to awards presentations is typically selected by stylists to complement the gowns and tuxedos they wear. Again, the product is on loan. By the year 2000, after it was well known that Gwyneth Paltrow's father bought her the diamond necklace she wore when she won her Oscar for Best Actress in *Shakespeare In Love*, symbols of Hollywood power changed. The biggest stars, such as Oprah Winfrey and Barbra Streisand, wore their own jewelry—jewels they had purchased themselves, not borrowed. When six- and seven-figure jewelry purchases are being made, the stars make the deals, not the stylists.

As the century turned, stars were beginning to reassess the value of stylists, the meaning of fashion, and the true meaning of power. Does Hollywood fashion power mean treating clothing like Katharine Hepburn did, wearing her gardening togs to a ceremony one year and a Calvin Klein ensemble another year? Is it time for Hollywood stars to start expressing themselves again? Is it time for the studios to start taking charge again? These are the fashion questions the new century will answer in time.

But why is the world watching how celebrities in Hollywood dress? Why do a billion viewers tune in for the Oscar presentation, and why do fashion editors around the world call it the biggest fashion show in the world? Is it because Hollywood represents instant communication and an instant way to

transmit new styles, new ways of dressing, new ways of looking at fashion as it affects culture?

At the end of the twentieth century, style was equated with the nonchalant glamour of California, and it was Hollywood that communicated that to the rest of the world, allowing second-hand jackets to top $500 jeans and $1,500 mules. As Tom Ford, the designer of the Gucci and Yves St. Laurent collections, noted: "The L.A. style of mid-century modernism has become a global trend."

But that isn't just a modern-day event. Remember Levi Strauss. Today, the two largest international apparel brands in the world—Levi Strauss, the inspiration of the ubiquitous jean, and The Gap, the maker and marketer of democratic fashion—have both risen from California. The high energy and excitement that has always emanated from California is refueled by its booming wave of surf culture, the lure of the entertainment industry, and the new technology of Silicon Valley. Fashion, like history, repeats itself in new guises and interpretations. It progresses as it regresses. It is as casual as it is dressed up, as democratic as it is elitist. It is a reflection of style that is lived every day in California. As designer Trina Turk said in *Los Angeles Magazine*, "When L.A. becomes the fashion capital of the world, everyone will talk about how all these trends started here. But we already know that."

*Opposite:* Julia Roberts at the L.A. Film Critics Awards, wearing an outfit by BCBG Max Azria.

Runway shot from a BCBG Max Azria show.

# BIOGRAPHIES

## CHAPTER 2

**Levi Strauss** came to California in 1853 to sell dry goods to gold miners. Jacob Davis suggested they make denim pants with rivets at stress points, and the first pair of jeans were constructed in 1873. The first wearers were miners and cowboys, but the world of clothes was changed forever.

**Nudie Cohn** got his start making G-strings for chorus girls (and others) in his Nudie's for Ladies shop on Broadway in Manhattan in the '30s, but he reached the stature of royalty in the world of Western wear. In 1947 Nudie's of Hollywood opened. Nudie made not only custom cowboy gear but also buttery Indian suedes, beaded dresses, pants, and chaps embroidered and decorated.

## CHAPTER 3

**Margit Fellegi**, the "first lady of swimwear," was the designer for Cole of California for more than 40 years. Fellegi revolutionized the swimwear industry with the introduction of Matletex—cotton with elastic thread to allow the fabric to stretch—and created a swimsuit to fit the contours of the body.

**Fred Cole** was a master of merchandising and promotion. He brought buyers and press from the East on his "Westward to the Sea," a deluxe train tour. When they arrived in Los Angeles, he wined and dined them and toured them around by limo. The grand finale was a fashion show and aquacade of his swimwear at the landmark Huntington Hotel in Pasadena.

**Anne Cole**, Fred's daughter, worked in the New York sales office to become a stylist and spokesperson. In 1982 Cole launched the Anne Cole Collection for women who were used to the style and quality of designer clothes (before designer swimwear).

**Mabs Barnes**, a discus thrower in the '32 Olympics, started Mabs of Hollywood with her husband, Wally Barnes, a former Olympic shot-putter and a salesman for the Van Raalte Co. (maker of underwear and girdles). He enlisted fellow 1932 Olympians as the sales team. The Mabs suit included a bias crotch, a patented leg design cut high around the front flexing muscle, which prevented wrinkling, riding up, and pulling. Her form-fitting maillot was without inner construction but had seaming that delineated the bustline. Mabs's innovations include two-way stretch suits, the use of California prints, printed satin Lastex, waterproof swimwear, a detachable uplift bra, and a concealed two-way front panel.

**Jo Lathwood** was a Santa Monica designer of playclothes and swimwear. She would design for swimwear companies, then disappear to the South Pacific for six months, where she found her inspiration.

She designed privately for clients including actresses Anne Baxter and Janet Gaynor.

**Mary Ann DeWeese**, Catalina's designer of the '40s, had many firsts to her credit: the jacquard sweater, appliquéd swimsuits, floral prints on stretch fabrics, and coordinated swimwear and playclothes. In 1951 she started DeWeese Designs, known for fit and construction. She designed the stretch strap, the Lasti-shir sundress, and the diving suits for the 1960 U.S. Olympic team. She is a true veteran of the swimwear market.

**Ed Stewart**, the Big Daddy of the swimsuit business, held showings of the Catalina line on Catalina Island. The "Giant White Steamer," officially the S.S. Catalina, would plow out of San Pedro harbor filled to the gunwales with buyers, press, fabric suppliers, and even Stewart's competitors.

**Bette Beck**, the daughter of Ed Stewart, created Elisabeth Stewart Swimwear in the 1950s with her husband and brothers. She was known for her classic swimwear.

**Rose Marie Reid** came to Hollywood from Canada in the late '40s and became the "glamour" swimsuit designer. To promote buying more than one suit, her ad slogan was, "One for the sea, one for the sun, and one for psychology." Her creations include a gold lamé suit, cocktail swimsuits (for parties and entertaining), the hourglass silhouette, velvets, beaded and exotic fabrics, and accessories such as stoles, jackets, and shirts.

CHAPTER 4

**Agnes Barrett** created not only the broomstick skirt but also the wrap-around skirt, originally made of sacking, which was immediately popular with American women. Her collection of understated casual dresses and sportswear for both active and spectator sports established her niche in the California market. Barrett was one of the eight Affiliated Fashionists.

**Louella Ballerino** created designs with a delicate balance between rustic and feminine, using fabric woven with chenille in the border for a skirt and combining it with an off-shoulder blouse. She studied crafts and designs that were distinctly Californian and Latino. She also created the dirndl dress.

**Addie Masters**, a Fashion Affiliate, started by designing dresses and then added glamorous at-home fashions. Her "Wrap Rascal," a casual, "easy-to-get-into" wrap dress, has been greatly copied.

**Dede Johnson** designed fashions that moved with the body without constricting it, reflecting her early interest in dance. She was nominated by *Sports Illustrated* for the American Sportswear design award for highest creativeness and inventiveness for her many fashion firsts. She also designed the sleeveless jacket (1949) and the band-top skirt (1960).

**Lou Van Roy** was one of the earliest designers of separates, created in response to the lean war years. Her slacks suits in 1936 were added to her collection of casual dresses.

**Viola Dimmitt** began her business making hand-appliquéd chiffon and satin dresses. Her covert cloth coat dress became a hit—it put her on the fashion weather map and started a trend toward more decorated rainwear.

**Juli Lynne Charlot** was steered by her theatrical family in the direction of the stage and film. But her talents as a fashion designer emerged when she decorated felt skirts with imaginative appliqués, creating her '50s poodle skirt.

**Faie Joyce** was a buyer for the Macy's shoe department in New York in the early 1940s, and it was the most talked-about shoe department in the city. Her next step was to start designing her own line. She and husband Bill Joyce, a Los Angeles shoe manufacturer, created a thriving business making handbags to match her fabric shoes worn with casual sportswear. She designed the first wedge shoe.

**Marjorie Montgomery** found new uses for fabrics such as mattress ticking and denim. In the 1940s her collection of cotton playclothes and dresses gained attention.She introduced the first three-piece playsuit and skirt under the label "Fireside Fashions," extending the life of playsuits by giving them an evening look.

**Jeri Holmes** presented her "Around the World in 80 Ways" at a press showing in Los Angeles. Begun in 1948 with husband Bill, under the Holmes of California label, Jeri's concept of an expandable wardrobe was born. Another first were her pre-packaged, "cut-and-sew" coordinates complete with directions for home sewers.

**Esprit**—This San Francisco company originated from the Plain Jane Dress Co., begun in the late 1960s by Jane Tise and friend Susie Russell, who sold dresses out of their car. When Russell married Doug Tompkins, he joined the company. When Jane retired in 1970, the company became Esprit de Corps and the focus turned to sportswear, with a young and fresh line. Esprit's nearby factory outlet was also a trendsetter.

CHAPTER 5

**Howard Greer** came to Hollywood in 1923 and is reputed to be the first person signed to a studio contract as costume designer (for Famous Players–Lasky). He was hired to design and create an image for the silent-film actress Pola Negri. In 1926 Greer opened his own salon. He retired in 1962 to write his memoirs, *Designing Male*, a witty look behind the scenes of early Hollywood.

**Max Factor** came to California in 1908, settling in downtown Los Angeles. He opened a barbershop in what was then the theater district, and he imported makeup and made hairpieces. In 1914 he perfected the first cream base makeup for motion pictures, and when color films began he created pancake makeup. Liquid makeup, lip gloss, concealers, and false eyelashes are all his innovations. In 1928 Factor moved to Hollywood to be closer to the film industry. Actresses could become "Max Factor Girls" for one dollar, and in return he promised to promote their films in his ads—virtually every actress or aspiring actress became a "Max Factor Girl." What began as a one-man barbershop is today an international name, marketing products in over 130 countries with sales of more than a billion dollars. The company is now owned by Proctor & Gamble.

**Travis Banton** followed Greer at Lasky (later Paramount) as head designer. One of the most talented and influential designers who dominated the screen through the '30s, he was the image-maker of Carole Lombard, Marlene Dietrich, and Mae West. In addition to his many film credits, he reorganized and integrated the Paramount wardrobe department. But his drinking binges made him hard to work with, and Paramount did not renew his contract in 1938. Banton moved on to Fox, Universal, and his own salon, but he never again achieved his early triumphs.

**Edith Head** ruled Paramount's wardrobe department from 1938 to 1967, when she moved to Universal. She worked on more than a thousand movies, was nominated for 35 Oscars, and won eight. She was also the fashion consultant for the Academy Awards from 1958 until 1970.

**Bernard Newman**, the custom designer at Bergdorf Goodman in New York, originally came to Hollywood in 1935 to design costumes for the RKO musical fashion film *Roberta* (which featured backless evening gowns similar to those seen on today's red carpets). Newman stayed on to create costumes for Ginger Rogers as she and Astaire danced their way through the hit films of the '30s and '40s.

**Jean Louis** was the head costume designer at Columbia Pictures in the '40s and '50s, creating glamorous gowns for beautiful women. The "femme fatale" dress worn by Ava Gardner in *The Killers* (1946), Rita Hayworth's famous *Gilda* dress, the chameleon chiffon for Marlene Dietrich's Las Vegas show, and the dress that Marilyn Monroe wore to sing "Happy Birthday" to President John F. Kennedy were all his creations. He was nominated 13 times for an Oscar and won in 1956.

**Adrian** was the great designer of Hollywood's Golden Age, and he became the icon of American fashion designers. Adrian's first screen credit, "Costumes by Adrian," was for Paramount's *Cobra*, starring Rudolph Valentino. His design career took off when Sid Grauman hired him to design costumes for the stage prologue of Charlie Chaplin's *Gold Rush* at Grauman's Chinese Theater in Hollywood. The next morning Adrian had seven offers, and he chose Cecil B. DeMille. In 1939 Adrian married actress Janet Gaynor (who had won, in 1927, the first Oscar presented to an actress), for whom Adrian had designed costumes for the 1930 film *Daddy Long Legs*. By 1940 Adrian was disenchanted with film, and he opened his own couture salon, Adrian Ltd., in 1942.

**Renie Conley** came to RKO as a sketch artist in the '20s and took the spotlight with her costumes for Ginger Rogers in the film *Kitty Foyle*. Knockoffs of the dress featured on the cover of *Life* magazine (December 1940) were sold at retail stores. Renie later joined Twentieth Century–Fox in 1960 and shared an Oscar for *Cleopatra* with Nino Novarese and Irene Sharaff in 1963.

**Irene** (Gibbons) had her own custom couture salon at Bullock's Wilshire, a first in retailing, with a following of celebrity customers. In 1942 she followed Adrian at MGM and became the executive designer. She designed for Marlene Dietrich, Greer Garson, Katharine Hepburn, Ingrid Bergman, Ginger Rogers, and Rosalind Russell. She returned to couture in 1947, winning the Neiman–Marcus Award for distinguished fashion. Irene's elegance extended from the hushed magnificence of her suits and day dresses to the subtle but grand sweep of her evening gowns.

**Helen Rose** was the costumer at MGM for more than twenty years. She won two Oscars, for *The Bad and the Beautiful* (1952), starring Lana Turner, and *I'll Cry Tomorrow* (1955), with Susan Hayward, and was nominated 12 times. Her pièce de résistance, however, was the gown she designed for the wedding of Grace Kelly to Prince Rainier in 1956.

**Elois Jenssen** was the original costume designer of *I Love Lucy* (1953–55 seasons, after which Edward Stevenson became the costumer). Jenssen shared an Oscar for *Samson and Delilah* in 1950; she was a founding member of the Costume Designers Guild and served as president. As Julia Earp, curator of the Universal studio's exhibition *Lucy: A Tribute*, writes: "*I Love Lucy* influenced fashion of the 1950s. It continues to define this period in America via reruns internationally. It is no accident that red hair was so popular in the '50s. . . . Her signature day dress, a polka-dot, three-quarter sleeve, fitted bodice with white bib and cuffs and full skirt, is immediately recognizable. This silhouette, along with the swing coat, maternity smocks, and scarves tied in your hair are always associated with her. Desilu marketed his-and-her matching pajama sets and a smoking jacket which they then wore on the show."

CHAPTER 6

**Don Loper**, suave and debonair, was considered a founding father of the Golden Boys. Among his most celebrated talents was the art of licensing, building an operation that was a model for similar operations of the future. By the '50s he had 11 product lines bearing his name, from small leather goods to boys' wear. Don Loper's limitless energy took him through an astounding array of artistic responsibilities as he moved through his career. MGM Studios gave him a multifaceted role, plus acting in a seven-year contract. But he was most famous for the screen clothes he designed. He later showed his custom collections in his beautiful home or at his Sunset Boulevard salon.

**Gus Tassell** came to California from Philadelphia to make seemingly simple styles but with subtly intricate cuts, in fabric contrasts that achieve shape by insinuation. Like his contemporaries, his clothes attracted a younger segment of affluent women. Although his earliest foray into commercial art was painting sideshow banners for his family's carnival business, he ultimately moved to New York in 1971 to design for the world renowned firm of Norman Norell after its namesake died. New York's high-fashion world adopted the California designer as one of its own, awarding him the American Fashion Critics Award in 1971 for his "serene purity of line and fashions which few designers in the world

are capable of achieving." He also won the International Silk Association Award and the National Cotton Council Award. But Tassell returned to Los Angeles where he continues to design.

**William Travilla** emerged from a motion-picture career to design a clothing line. He originally chose to open his headquarters on the west side of the city, although much later he moved to the downtown marketplace. Even as he developed his wholesale high-fashion business, he continued to design for many productions on the large and small screens. He designed numerous dresses for Marilyn Monroe (*The Seven Year Itch*, *Gentlemen Prefer Blondes*) as well as designing for the TV series *Dallas*. He won an Academy Award for his costume designs in the film *The Adventures of Don Juan*. A California native, born in Avalon on Catalina Island, Travilla was an avid sportsman. The company he founded bearing his name continues today.

**William Pearson** came on the scene in 1960 with a talent for making dresses for both daytime through evening look simple but elegant. He chose to remain in the downtown market area of Los Angeles, where he had his showroom and workrooms. His clothes were strictly "off-the-rack," not as expensive as those of the rest of the Golden Boys, but with quiet good taste. He was notorious within his company for working for months preparing a new collection, only to chuck it at the eleventh hour, working the staff at a frenzied pace to be ready for the scheduled (or rescheduled) showing. He always pulled it together, impeccably coordinated at zero hour. Typically Pearson, he took a crash course in French, abruptly closed his business, and left for a four-year hiatus in Paris. There he worked for couturier Christian Dior, before returning to Los Angeles and reopening his own business.

**Paul Whitney**, a graduate of the Art Institute of Chicago, spent two years in Paris as a sketch artist for Jacques Fath and Elsa Schiaparelli. In 1957 he came to Los Angeles to open his own high-fashion business. His hallmark is a crisp, uncluttered line for daytime and glamorous evening clothes.

**Michael Novarese** is a favorite on the trunk-show circuit in upscale specialty stores. His buttery Memphis drawl has charmed affluent customers ever since he opened his business in 1959. His luxurious cocktail and evening dresses have been on the backs of the social elite across the country for more than three decades.

**David Hayes**, a latter-day Golden Boy, also has a theatrical background. His collections feature a clean-cut, classic style, using lightweight wools (such as double-face wools), silks, and linens perfect for the California climate. Hayes's

clothes are most popular with the "ladies who lunch." David Hayes label-collectors include Sharon Stone and Sophia Loren. Recently he extended his fashion reach with three new labels—David Hayes Collection, David Hayes Accessories, and David Hayes Sportswear—and opened a boutique in Palm Desert.

**Jack Hansen** opened one of the first Beverly Hills boutiques, Jax, in 1950 and specialized in tight pants and snug T-shirts. "We showed a girl's fanny for the first time. Frankly, the only people who should wear my pants are the string beans . . . the long-legged, slim-hipped girls. All their lives they've been a skinny nothing and suddenly they're a chic something." Jack, a savvy avant-garde merchant, featured the designs of a new up-and-coming designer, Rudi Gernreich.

**Rudi Gernreich**, the visionary, futuristic designer, created a see-through shirt that exposed the breasts and predicted that swimwear would be topless within five years. In 1964 the fashion editor of *Look* magazine asked Rudi to actually design a suit to fit his prediction. To Rudi's surprise, retailers placed orders for the topless swimsuit. (Three thousand topless suits sold at $25.) Rudi will be recognized forever as the space-age designer who captured the look of the '60s, but his impact is not contained to that decade: he liberated women from clothes that constrained the

body and created the first unisex looks.

**Jimmy Galanos** was a master of the "little nothing" dress, usually low necked, made of wool jersey or crepe, draped for slimming the body, and accented with a single piece of jewelry. Galanos is best known for his cocktail and smocked chiffon evening dresses, wool crepes and jerseys draped or cut on the bias, and for the pairing of unusual fabrics. Galanos developed many loyal celebrity customers, including Marlene Dietrich, Loretta Young, Rosalind Russell, Abbe Lane, and Diana Ross. He ventured into Hollywood film at the request of Rosalind Russell, a friend who loved his clothes. Galanos made both of Nancy Reagan's inaugural ball gowns and the two earlier gowns she wore as California's First Lady. He won the Coty Award in 1956 (and entered the Coty Hall of Fame in 1959), the Stanley Award in 1986, an award from the Council of Fashion Designers of America in 1985. The Los Angeles County Museum of Art has held two retrospectives of his work. He retired in 1998.

CHAPTER 7

**Linda Gravenites** was the Haight-style guru, seamstress, and earth mother who turned out clothes and costumes for Janis Joplin. She remembers, "It was an exciting time. Imagine what you wanted to do—and do it—*anything* was possible. People dressed for fun. We were dressing up to have a grand time and to be looked at. We got pretty scathing when hip didn't come from the soul."

**Jessica McClintock** began as a flower-power designer in the '60s, but today she is known for romantic prom dresses and evening dresses, which are sold in the company's 27 boutiques and specialty stores; the company also has its own Rodeo Drive salon. Gunne Sax, now the junior line, Jessica McClintock Bridal, Jessica McClintock Girls, Scott McClintock (missy division), and Jessica McClintock Designer are all under the corporate banner. To quote the designer: "I built this myself. I didn't think it was work because I loved it so much."

## CHAPTER 8

**Hoffman Fabrics International—** Through their love of surfing, surfers Walt and Phil Hoffman influenced the fabric and design of the company founded by their father, Rube. Walt's daughter, Joyce, was a six-time women's world champion surfer in the '60s. Phil has the largest collection of long boards in the U.S. The brothers create fabric style and technology for the boardwear industry. The company has a large archive of old, authentic Hawaiian textiles dating back to the early '50s. Hoffman has printing facilities throughout Asia and a hand-batik factory in Bali.

**Duke Boyd** founded Hang Ten in 1952 and became the surfing patriarch of marketing, merchan-

dising, and licensing of lifestyle sportswear. Probably the most important single event that moved Hang Ten into mainstream fashion was embroidering the logo on the front of the trunks. His product placement progressed from surf shops, the backbone of beach lifestyle, to department stores many miles from the water.

**Jack O'Neill** pioneered the wetsuit in the late '50s, and through research and technology he created the super suit for the Navy Seals in the '60s and the urethane surf leash and split-toe booties for surfers. Today O'Neill International (run by Jack's six children) markets wetsuits for men, women, and children, accessories, sportswear, boardwear, and surfboards around the world. The company is researching a "hot patch" of niacin to keep the body warm and niacin fabrics for wetsuit linings.

**Quiksilver International USA—** In 1976 surfers Bob McKnight and Jeff Hakman started Quiksilver, the largest surfwear company, in Surf City (Huntington Beach, California). Quiksilver was named after the Quicksilver Messenger Service band. Surfing had been a macho sport until Gidget and women's surf competition in the 1960s, but not until the '90s did girls really start surfing. Surfwear manufacturers such as Quiksilver now promote women surfers on the pro tour. Quiksilver recently moved in skateboard territory with the purchase of Tony Hawk.

## CHAPTER 9

**Bob Mackie**, a native Californian, has designed for movies, stage, nightclub acts, and television, and his ready-to-wear company has licensed home furnishings, menswear, furs, jewelry, accessories, and fragrances. Mackie's credits include the *Sonny and Cher Comedy Hour*, *The Carol Burnett Show*, and Cher's *Believe* concert tour. He has been nominated for 15 Emmys and has won seven, and he was nominated for three Oscars. In 1999 the Fashion Institute of Technology in New York held a Mackie retrospective.

**BCBG/Max Azria**—"Bon Chic Bon Genre" is French slang for "good style, good fashion." The label is designed by Azria's wife, Lubova. BCBG clothes have been seen on television shows such as *Friends*, *Seinfeld*, *Ally McBeal*, and *Entertainment Tonight* as well as on celebrity customers Sharon Stone, Ashley Judd, Uma Thurman, Madonna, and Minnie Driver. BCBG now includes BCBG Contemporary, three junior lines, licensed shoes, handbags, sunglasses, swimwear, menswear, and 65 BCBG boutiques in the U.S., Asia, and Paris. In 1998 Azria acquired the French couture house Hervé Léger and its flagship store in Paris.

**Richard Tyler**, an Australian, came to Los Angeles in 1984. Lisa Trafficante became his wife and business partner, and in 1987 they founded Tyler Trafficante, Inc., to market Tyler's menswear designs. They opened a boutique and two years later added a women's line. In 1993–94 he designed the Anne Klein collection, keeping his signature studio in Los Angeles. He won the Costume Fashion Designers of America Award for his signature collections in 1993, 1994, and 1995. Tyler began his Silver Screen collection in 1995, and his client list includes Julia Roberts, Meg Ryan, Laura Dern, Angelica Huston, Nicole Kidman, Winona Ryder, and Janet Jackson. From 1996–98 Tyler was design director of the Italian fashion house Byblos, designing both women's and men's collections. He started Richard Tyler shoes for men and women and won the Michelangelo Shoe Award in 1996. He made a licensing agreement with Gruppo Nadini to produce the Richard Tyler Collection, a sportswear line. His menswear collection, Bespoken, is also produced in Italy. Richard Tyler Couture is produced in Los Angeles workrooms, and all work is "in-house."

**Trina Turk** started her own line of clothing in 1995, based in Los Angeles. Her clothes, known for their casual fit and fun prints, are popular with Hollywood stars such as Julia Roberts, Gwen Stefani, Hilary Swank, Katie Holmes, and Heather Graham, and are featured on numerous television shows.

# BIBLIOGRAPHY

*Books*

Bailey, Margret J. *Those Glamour Years.* Secarcud, New Jersey: Citadel Press, 1982

Bradley, Barry. *Galanos.* Cleveland: Western Reserve Historical Society, 1996.

Brand, Tyler. *100 Years of Western Wear.* Salt Lake City: Gibbs-Smith, 1993.

Calistro, Paddy. *Edith Head's Hollywood.* New York: E.P. Dutton, 1983.

DeCaro, Frank, *Unmistakably Mackie.* New York: Universe Publishing, 2000.

Faure, Jacques. *Rudi Gernreich: A Retrospective.* Los Angeles: Los Angeles Fashion Group, 1985.

Fox, Patty. *Star Style at the Academy Awards.* Santa Monica, California: Angel City Press, 2000.

Greer, Howard. *The Designing Male.* New York: Putnam, 1949.

Heinman, Jim. *Out with the Stars.* New York: Abbeville Press, 1987.

Hersh, Pauline, ed. *Journal of the Southern California Jewish Historical Society*: Legacy, Vol. 1, No. 2, Spring 1988.

Hoskyn, Barney. *Beneath a Diamond Sky, Haight Ashbury 1965–1970.* New York: Simon & Schuster, 1997.

International Fashion Group , Los Angeles: fashion show program, *Those Designing Women—Those Golden Years 1935–1955.* International Fashion Group , Los Angeles, 1976.

Kampion, Drew. *Stoked, A History of Surf Culture.* Santa Monica, California: General Publishing, 1997.

Kyser, Jack, Chief Economist. *Los Angeles Economic Development Corp. Apparel Industry Profile*: Table 2, Textile Manufacturing Employment; Table 4, Textile Manufacturing Jobs; Table 5, Textile Manufacturing Dollar Volume (1998 Estimates).

Law, Lisa. *Flashing on the Sixties.* San Francisco: Chronicle Books, 1987.

Lee, Sara Tamerlin. *American Fashion, The Life and Lines of Adrian, Mainbocher, McCardell, Norell and Trigere.* New York: Quadrangle/New York Times Books, 1975

Leese, Elizabeth. *Costume Design in Movies.* New York: Dover, 1991.

Lobenthal, Joe. *Radical Rags, Fashion of the Sixties.* New York: Abbeville Press, 1990.

Maeder, Edward. *Hollywood and History: Costume Design in Film.* Los Angeles: Thames & Hudson, Los Angeles County Museum of Art, 1987.

McConathy, Dale. *Hollywood Costume—Glamour Glitter! Romance.* New York: Harry N. Abrams, 1976.

McKay, Agnes. *California Fashion Trends.* Vol. 1, No. 2, Feb. 1947, 21–59.

Moffitt, Peggy, Marylou Luther, and William Claxton. *The Rudi Gernreich Book.* New York: Rizzoli, 1991.

Mouse, Stanley. *Freehand: The Art of Stanley Mouse.* Berkeley, California: SL9 Books, 1993.

Rose, Phil. *20 Years Less 8%.* Los Angeles: The Fashion Press, 1960.

Stoddard, John. *John Stoddard's Lectures, So. California.* Vol. X.

Boston: Balch Brothers Co., 1898.

*Textile Association of Los Angeles Directory*, 1998.

Wolman, Baron. *Classic Rock and Other Rollers*. Santa Rosa, California: Squarebooks, 1992.


## Periodicals

Abcarian, Robin, "Fashion's new frontier," *Los Angeles Times Magazine*, Aug. 22, 1999.

——, "Galanos cuts loose," *Los Angeles. Times Magazine*, Sept. 12, 1999.

Bloomberg News, *Los Angeles Times Business*, "Authentic Fitness to be sold to Warnaco for $435 million," Nov. 17, 1999.

Collins, Amy Fine, "Anything for Oscar," Edith Head, *Vanity Fair*, March 1999.

Costin, Glynis, and Jennifer Wilson, "L.A. style—move over Paris," *Los Angeles Magazine*, Sept. 1999.

Cover story on Ginger Rogers in *Kitty Foyle* dress designed by Renie Conley, *Life*, December 9, 1940.

Earnest, Leslie, "Surf & Turf—Hilfiger wades into niche market with insiders help," *Los Angeles Times*, May 30, 1999.

Earnest, Leslie, "Quicksilver takes a new wave approach," *Los Angeles Times*, Oct. 29, 1999.

"50 years of Hollywood Fashion," *In Style*, Fall 1997.

Herman-Cohen, Valli, "Oscars: The Ultimate Advertisement," *Los Angeles Times*, March 24, 2000.

Horyn, Cathy, "The shock heard round the world," *Vanity Fair*, May 1998.

Jacobs, Laura, "Glamour by Adrian," *Vanity Fair*, June 2000.

"Jax's, he shows you the girl!," *Life*, Oct. 8, 1965.

Johnson, Greg, "Jeans war, survival of the fittest," *Los Angeles Times*, Dec. 3, 1998.

Johnson, Greg, "Levi ads wear on competitors," *Los Angeles Times*, May 5, 1998.

Jones, Robert A., "Now Comes the Beach," *Los Angeles Times*, July 12, 1998.

Lee, Louis, "A savory captain for Old Navy," *Business Week*, Nov. 8, 1999.

"Levi Strauss taps Pepsi marketer," *Los Angeles Times*, Sept. 8, 1999.

Mann, William, "Costume design: Travis Banton, dressing screen legends of the 1930s," *Architectural Digest*, April 1996.

Michener, Charles, "Bill Blass rhymes with class," *Town and Country*, Sept. 1999.

Mink, Nina, "How Levi trashed a great American brand," *Fortune*, April 12, 1999.

Naridoza, Ed, ed., "California, a style is born," *Women's Wear Daily*, California Supplement, Fairchild, Aug. 1999.

Prouty, Judy, "An Oscar Fashion Flashback," *Los Angeles Times Magazine*, March 21, 1999.

Reuters, "Warnaco offers $420 million for clothes maker," *Los Angeles Times*, Oct. 11, 1999.

Rourke, Mary, "Where to next?," *Los Angeles Times*, Aug. 20, 1993.

Ryan, Thomas, "Gap's $1 billion budget to fund growth ads" *Women's Wear Daily*, April 6, 1999.

Scallon, Virginia, *California Stylist*; "25 Years of Fashion", Vol. XXVI, No. 4, April, 1962.

"The first family of surfing, the Paskowitz's are the coolest guys on the beach," *New York Times*, Aug. 23, 1999.

Thomas, Dana, "Screen gems," *New York Times*, April 1997.

*Touring Topics*, "Club run to Malibu Ranch," Automobile Club of Southern California, May 1910.

Tyler, Tim, "California here it comes," *Time Magazine*, Nov. 7, 1969.

*Vogue's View*, "Galanos Glitter," *Vogue*, April 1998.

Wells, Melanie, "Entrepreneur as stunt man," *Forbes*, Nov. 1, 1999.

*Women's Wear Daily*, "Junior streetwear report," April 1, 1999.

# PHOTO CREDITS

Courtesy the Academy of Motion Picture Arts and Sciences: 21, 26 (top and bottom), 27, 39, 56 (left), 64, 78, 79, 83, 86 (left), 87, 89 (top and bottom), 90 (top), 93 (right), 94, 96, 97; © AFP/CORBIS: 155, 160 (left and right, photo Peter Morgan), 165; Bette Beck: 56 (center); Courtesy Dianne Biedman: 46; Courtesy Billabong: 150; © Randy Bloomfield/oi2.com: 2–3; Body Glove: 54; Courtesy Duke Boyd: 145 (bottom); Eddie Brandt: 88; Photo Grant Brittian: 153; Courtesy Bruce Brown: 151; Courtesy Michael Butler: 132; California Fashion Creators: 1; Paddy Calistro: 85; Courtesy Capitol Records/Beach Boys: 147; Marge Carne: 50; Photo Bill Claxton: 53, 119; Patty Clayton: 107 (background); Photo Henry Diltz: 122, 123, 124, 125, 126–27,

135; Courtesy Gene Autry Museum: 29 (right); Getty Images: 34 (Prouser/Reuters), 35 (left and right, Papi/Reuters), 51 (Gene Lester/Hulton Archive), 55, 57 (right, Christensen/Reuters), 130 (Hulton Archive), 161 (right, Reuters); Globe Photos: 154, 164 (photo Fitzroy Barrett); Courtesy Linda Gravenites: 128 (photo Jeff Hettinger); Marian Hall Collection: 6–7 (Pictorial California), 8 (Union Pacific), 10, 12–13, 14 (photo John Miehle), 15 (photo Art Strele), 38 (left, Keystone), 38 (right), 44, 67, 73 (left), 82, 86 (background), 90 (bottom); David Hayes: 106 (right); International Fashion Group, Los Angeles: 42 (left), 56 (right), 60, 66, 70, 75; International Fashion Group, New York: 107 (right), 116; Jantzen: 68–69; Photo Lisa Law: 120–21, 136; Courtesy Levi Strauss & Co. Archives: 20–21, 22 (right), 25; Los Angeles Library, Herald Examiner Collection: 117; Bob Mackie: 159 (photo Harry Langdon); Courtesy Holly Mitchell: 102; Courtesy Jimmy Mitchell: 49 (photo Tommy Mitchell), 57 (right), 58–59, 63, 71 (photo Tommy Mitchell), 80, 112 (photo Tommy Mitchell); Courtesy Sheri Mobley: 42 (right), 43; Stanley Mouse: 131; Courtesy O'Neill: 142–43 (photo Brian Bielmann), 144; J. Orsi: 57 (center); Courtesy Otis College of Art and Design: 110–11, 111 (both, photo Berliner Studio); Photofest: 17, 33, 40, 41, 47, 73 (right), 76–77, 91, 93 (left), 98, 104, 105, 133, 134, 148, 156

(left and right), 158; PictureQuest: 4–5 ("Sunset and Water," © Larry Brownstein); John Post: 18; Courtesy Dan Price: 9 (left and right); Oreste Pucciani: 52; Courtesy Joe Quigg: 145 (top); Quiksilver: cover and 140–41 (photo Jim Russi), 152; Courtesy Reagan Library: 30–31; Courtesy Dave Rochlen: 146; Courtesy Rosebudmedia.com: 21 (photo Fergus Greer); Courtesy Roy Rogers & Dale Evans Museum: 29 (left); Santa Inez Historical Society: 22 (left); Reprinted with the permission of The Saturday Evening Post, © 1916–1963 Curtis Publishing Company, Courtesy Norman Rockwell Estate: 24; Courtesy Edwina Shaff: 95; Courtesy Joe Simms: 92 (photo Bill Cunningham); Photo Victor Skrebneski: 109; Courtesy Speedo International Limited: 54–55; Photo Bert Stern, Courtesy of Vogue, Condé Nast Publications, Inc.: 138 (Vogue, 3/15/1969); Courtesy Sunset Magazine: 11; © Time Inc.: 99 (Bob Landry/Life Magazine), 100–101 (Gordon Parks/Life Magazine); Courtesy Trina Turk: 162 (photo Jonathan Skow); Courtesy Richard Tyler: 161 (left); Courtesy Paul Whitney: 106 (left); Photo Baron Wolman: 28, 128–29; Courtesy June Wylie: 48; Courtesy Xoxo: 139 (photo Lasdaba/DeCarlo); Photo Christa Zinner: endpapers and 36–37, 108, 113, 114, 115 (left and right), 118

# Acknowledgments

A special thanks to:

Paddy Calistro—truly an angel of Angel City Press, without whose advice and guidance this book would not have been published.

Mary Norton—friend indeed, who cheered all the way—our reader!

Dan Price—Hollywood historian, film buff, who loves to share old Hollywood.

Sheri Mobley—Mobley Communications, Public Relations, who knows how and where to find anyone in the fashion world.

Julia Earp—researcher and *Lucy* historian with great enthusiasm!

Justine Mandelbaum—librarian who combed the resource center at The Fashion Institute of Design and Merchandising on our behalf.

Aimee McDaniel—our computer whiz.

Carol Cavella—for helping us wrap this up.

Jimmy Mitchell—for her generous support and for sharing photos.

Ruth Peltason—who believed in our book.

Christa Zinner—photographer and artist as seen in her photographs.

Eric Himmel—editor-in-chief with great patience.

Julie Alvarez, Leah Arroyo, Jenny Aspell, Sue Barry, Bette Beck, Lenore Benson, Bob Berg, Suzanne Bergstrom, Richard Battaglia, Elizabeth and Duke Boyd, Kay Boyer, Liz Brady, Steve Branch, Jamie Branagen, Rosemary Brantley, Barbara Broudo, California Fashion Creators, Debbie Call, Nicholas Callaway, Lucy Campbell, Nadine Dee Carvasi, Pat Claytor, Barbara Cohn, Carolyn Cole, The Colleagues, Jill Davidson, Carmen Deforest, Carol De Long, Joan Deignau, Lynn Downey, Tom Doyle, Joanne Drake, Christian Dystra, Fashion Institute of Design and Merchandising, Patty Fox, Jimmy Galanos, Mickey Gillian, Bridget Gorin, Linda Gravenites, Marie Gray, Delores Greer, Maury Hall, Adam Hall, Ben Hall, Peter Hall, Chad Hayes, Jeanette Alexander Hyland, International Fashion Group, Beverly Jackson, Jantzen, Inc., Larry Karman, Randy King, Dorothy Kistler, Eleanor La Vove, Pilar Laws, Larry Lazalo, Maryon Lears, Sharon Lee, Maurice Levin, Luna, Gordon McClelland, Christian McEntee, Bob Mackie, John Marin, Holly Mitchell, Joan Mitchell, Maggie Murray, Robert Nelson, Martha Nielsen, Michael Novarese, Vickie Pass, Steve and Debbie Pezman, Alison Poulsen, Vickie Pouré, Jeff Reidel, Mary Lou Roberts, David Rochlen, Nick Rodionoff, Roy Rogers, Jr., Sandy Rosenbaum, Bill Sarris, Alex Schraff, Steven Sebolt, Alan Seymour, Edwina Shaff, Cameron Silver, Joe Simms, Lester Sloan, Craig Steycek, Kathy Sullivan, Ellen Sweony, Gus Tassell, Sharon Tate, Jeanne Taylor, Jack Watte, Beth & John Weingarten, Paul Whitney, Mary Jane Wick, Jenny Wilson, Shirley Wilson, Baron Wolman, June Wylie, and Morgan Yates.

# About the Authors

**Marian Hall** began her career in the fashion office as a model at Bullock's Wilshire and later at Bullock's Pasadena. She became a manufacturer of maternity and preteen clothes in the 1950s and '60s and worked as fashion stylist for the lingerie firm the Olga Company, before joining the Fashion Institute of Design and Merchandising in Los Angeles as curator of its costume museum. She has served on the boards of the International Fashion Group, Los Angeles, the Costume Council of the Los Angeles County Museum of Art, and the Colleagues, a charitable organization. A native Californian, she resides in Malibu.

**Marjorie Carne** was fashion director of the California Fashion Creators, an association of designers and manufacturers, then executive vice president. She initiated the annual California Press Week and worked as regional director of the International Fashion Group, Los Angeles. Most recently, she has served as executive director of the Coalition of Apparel Industries in California and as secretary/treasurer of Designers at the Essex House in New York. She resides in Glendale, California.

**Sylvia Sheppard** was an editor at *Women's Wear Daily* in New York until she was transferred to Los Angeles to be the West Coast editor. She later worked as fashion and sales promotion director for Bullock's Sherman Oaks in southern California and went on to become assistant fashion director at the Broadway Stores. After several years, she joined the Fashion Institute of Design and Merchandising in Administration. She served as regional director of the International Fashion Group, Los Angeles, and is currently its executive administrator. She resides in La Crescenta, California.

Project Manager: Eric Himmel
Editor: Nicole Columbus
Designer: Darilyn Lowe Carnes
Additional Photo Research: Kevin Kwan

Library of Congress Control Number: 2001134049
ISBN 0–8109–1013–6

Printed in Hong Kong and bound in China
10 9 8 7 6 5 4 3 2 1

 Harry N. Abrams, Inc.
100 Fifth Avenue
New York, N.Y. 10011
www.abramsbooks.com

Abrams is a subsidiary of LA MARTINIÈRE GROUPE